MW00583443

Twin Peaks

TV Milestones Series

General Editor
Barry Keith Grant, Brock University

TV Milestones is part of the Contemporary Approaches to Film and Media Series.

A complete listing of the books in this series can be found online at wsupress.wayne.edu

TWIN PEAKS

Julie Grossman
and Will Scheibel

TV MILESTONES SERIES

Wayne State University Press   Detroit

ISBN 978-0-8143-4622-8 (paperback)
ISBN 978-0-8143-4623-5 (e-book)

Library of Congress Control Number: 2019942120

Wayne State University Press
Leonard N. Simons Building
4809 Woodward Avenue
Detroit, Michigan 48201-1309

Visit us online at wsupress.wayne.edu

This book is dedicated to Phil Novak and Andrea Scheibel,
who live with us in "the absurd mystery of
the strange forces of existence."

CONTENTS

ACKNOWLEDGMENTS

I t was a pleasure to work with Wayne State University Press ix and especially Marie Sweetman, our acquisitions editor, whose warmth and expert guidance helped us immeasurably through the publication process. Annie Martin, the editor-in-chief, was our first contact at the press and pointed us in the right directions. Barry Keith Grant, the series editor of "TV Milestones," and our anonymous readers offered useful insights that were important to our revisions. The Noreen Reale Falcone Library at Le Moyne College and the Ernest Stevenson Bird Library at Syracuse University aided us in conducting research together in Syracuse, New York. Our department chairs—at Le Moyne, Maura Brady in English and Michael Streissguth in Communication and Film Studies, and at Syracuse, Erin Mackie in English—supported our work on this project. Will would also like to thank the College of Arts and Sciences at Syracuse for granting him a semester of sabbatical leave. The students in our classes on film noir and *Twin Peaks* shared in our fascination with this series as both scholars and fans. We were able to present portions of chapters at conferences organized by the Association of Adaptation Studies, the Literature/Film Association, and the Modernist Studies Association. Agents Discenza and

El Younsi assisted in our research, while David Israel (the CEO of TwinPeaksTour.com) drove us to filming locations in Washington and gave deeply knowledgeable commentary. In addition, we are grateful to the following friends and colleagues, some of whom are *Twin Peaks* fans themselves and all of whom provided encouragement and fun distractions as we wrote: Amy Breiger, Steve Cohan, Bryan Cole, Kelly Delevan, Matt Fee, Jim Fleury, Mike Goode, Eric Grode, Roger Hallas, Jim Hannan, Chris and Kate Hanson, Tom Leitch, Linda LeMura, Joe Marina, Kyle Meikle, Barton Palmer, Jolynn Parker, Kendall Phillips, Ann Ryan, Eevie Smith, Matt Spitzmueller, Kate Costello-Sullivan, Zachary Snow, Tim Sullivan, Farha Ternikar, Travis Vande Berg, Con Verevis, Kim Waale, Patrick Williams, and Bob and Dawn Wilson. Special thanks to William Twede from Twede's Café in North Bend, Washington for great conversation and being an ally of this project.

Introduction

A Short Production and Reception History

On Sunday, April 8, 1990, the day the *Twin Peaks* pilot premiered on ABC, the *New York Times* ran a full-page advertisement with a giant pull quote from a review in the British luxury lifestyle magazine *Connoisseur*: "*Twin Peaks*—the series that will change TV." Quotes followed from seven other reviewers making similar pronouncements based on advanced screenings of the pilot (Advertisement for *Twin Peaks* H30). The series has since been credited with influencing the science fiction-FBI procedural *The X-Files* (Fox, 1993–2002), the myth-building mystery *Lost* (ABC, 2004–10), and the detective drama *The Killing* (AMC, 2011–13; Netflix, 2014) about the "ripple effects of a crime"—a "murder-of-girl-next-door-with-secret-sordid-life," no less—in the Pacific Northwest. One list cites these in addition to seventeen other titles (Tobias et al.). Episodes in series such as *The Simpsons* (Fox, 1989–present) and *Sesame Street* (PBS, 1969–present) have spoofed and paid homage to *Twin Peaks*, ensuring its canonicity in popular culture.[1] As the *New York Times* advertisement illustrates, though, ABC actually presold the series as a television milestone.

Initially, the network reaped the benefits of such a promotional campaign (and the word-of-mouth marketing it generated). When the two-hour pilot aired at 9:00 p.m. EST, an increasing number of viewers tuned in every half hour, reaching a total audience of around thirty-five million (a 33 percent market share, or a third of the people watching television from 9:00 to 11:00 p.m.) (Hughes 118). A midseason replacement, the first season of *Twin Peaks* ran for seven episodes on Thursdays at 9:00 p.m. opposite *Cheers* (NBC, 1982–93), part of NBC's formidable "Must See TV" lineup, and Episode 1 garnered the highest ratings ABC had seen in four years during that time slot (Carter D8). ABC's senior vice president of research partly attributed its success to the "water cooler syndrome" (i.e., around the office watercooler, people will talk about the previous night's episode of a memorable series) (D8).

Cocreators Mark Frost and David Lynch first met in 1986 through their mutual agent, Tony Krantz. Prior to developing *Twin Peaks*, they wrote a script for a feature film titled *Venus Descending*, an adaptation of Anthony Summers's book *Goddess: The Secret Lives of Marilyn Monroe* (1985), but United Artists terminated the project, anxious about its implication of Bobby Kennedy in Monroe's death (Lynch and McKenna 241–42). Next was a comedy for De Laurentiis Entertainment Group starring Steve Martin and Martin Short titled *One Saliva Bubble*, which *Twin Peaks* contributing writer Robert Engels later described as a film "about an electric bubble from a computer that bursts over this town and changes people's personalities" (Rodley 155). Six weeks before shooting started, Dino De Laurentiis informed them that the company was bankrupt and being dissolved (Lynch and McKenna 243). Finally, Frost and Lynch pitched a series to NBC about FBI agents hunting down the survivors of the mythical sunken continent of Lemuria— hence the title, *The Lemurians*. While the network wanted them to make it as a film, Lynch felt it would only work as a series, and *The Lemurians* never went any further (247).

Lynch claims that the idea for *Twin Peaks* came to him and Frost, sitting in a Du-par's coffee shop in Los Angeles, with the "image of a body washing up on the shore of a lake" (Rodley 157). After completing a first draft of the script for the pilot, they pitched *Twin Peaks* to ABC in December of 1988, calling it *Northwest Passage* (a title that already belonged to a 1940 film adaptation of Kenneth Roberts's historical novel of the same name set in the French and Indian War). Shooting the pilot commenced in February of the following year (Hughes 106). Part of the inspiration derived from the 1908 murder of Hazel Irene Drew in the town of Sand Lake, New York, where Frost spent his childhood summer vacations and heard local legends about the unsolved case (Bushman and Givens E1).

Principal photography took place in Washington, mostly outside of Seattle in Snoqualmie, North Bend, and Fall City. Poulsbo, Washington, provided the shore on which Laura Palmer's body was discovered wrapped in plastic. After a cold twenty-two-and-a-half days of filming, the cast and crew returned to Los Angeles to shoot interior scenes in a San Fernando Valley warehouse and other exteriors in the Malibu woods (Lynch and McKenna 251–52).[2] Casting brought a wide range of different actors to the series: attractive young newcomers poised for stardom Sherilyn Fenn, Lara Flynn Boyle, Mädchen Amick, Dana Ashbrook, and James Marshall; older television stars Michael Ontkean from *The Rookies* (ABC, 1972–76) and Peggy Lipton from *The Mod Squad* (ABC, 1968–73); Hollywood veterans Russ Tamblyn and Richard Beymer from *West Side Story* (1961) and three-time Academy Award nominee Piper Laurie, best known for *The Hustler* (1961)[3]; Eric DaRe, son of actor Aldo Ray and the series' casting director Johanna Ray; and members of Lynch's film repertoire Kyle MacLachlan, Jack Nance, Catherine Coulson, and Charlotte Stewart. Danish television scholar Andreas Halskov introduces the useful term "intertextual casting strategy" to describe Lynch's approach to selecting actors (65).[4]

Relatively unknown actors played characters who became increasingly central to the story as it continued, especially into

Twin Peaks: The Return (subsequently *The Return*) in 2017. Amputee actor Al Strobel, for instance, delivered a compelling performance as spiritual guide MIKE, alternately called Philip Gerard and the "One-Armed Man" in references to an actor and character, respectively, from *The Fugitive* (ABC, 1963–67). Painter, sculptor, and activist Michael Horse, a Yaqui descendent, played Deputy Hawk, whom Horse described as "one of the best characters, I think, ever written for television." Speaking to the dearth of roles available to Native Americans, Horse has said, "both as an artist and as a tribal person, I'm extremely proud of that character" ("Postcards").

Although Frost and Lynch wrote a story arc to satisfy network executives, they left it general enough to allow for a kind of organic approach to the storytelling in the series (Rodley 162). For example, Lynch explains that he cast the late Frank Silva as BOB after shooting a scene for the pilot in Laura's bedroom. Silva, a set dresser, was moving furniture and accidently blocked the doorway with a chest of drawers. Upon hearing someone say, "Frank, don't lock yourself in that room," Lynch decided to get a shot of Silva crouched behind the bars at the foot of Laura's bed. When shooting a later scene in the living room with Grace Zabriskie as Laura's distraught mother, Sarah, Lynch accidentally caught Silva's reflection in the mirror (164). BOB entered the story when ABC required Frost and Lynch to create a "closed" ending for the pilot to be released on video in the United Kingdom as a stand-alone feature film in case the series was not picked up. Lynch's footage of Silva thus proved fortuitous. Released five months before its US television debut and almost a year before airing in the United Kingdom, the extended version of the pilot identified BOB as Laura's killer, a figure whom Sarah could see in visions, and then flashed forward twenty-five years into the future with Laura reappearing in the Red Room (Hughes 116–17). Seemingly arbitrary, perhaps, in the context of the pilot, this somewhat improvised "solution" to the mystery actually opened subsequent storylines involving demonic possession and interdimensional spaces. Frost and Lynch formally introduced BOB in Episode 1 and recontextualized much of the footage for the extended ending in Cooper's dream at the end of Episode 2.

Despite a core base of loyal fans, ratings for *Twin Peaks* gradually declined over the first season as Frost and Lynch protracted any semblance of closure on Laura's murder, ending the first season on yet another cliffhanger (the season finale aired on a Wednesday night, the first of several confusing scheduling changes). In October of 1990, ABC moved the series to Saturday nights for the second season—foreclosing any "watercooler" effect—and critics started turning on the series they had championed mere months earlier (Hughes 117–18). ABC announced it would go on "indefinite hiatus" on February 15, 1991, and Lynch came on *Late Night with David Letterman* (CBS, 1982–93) asking fans to write to the president of ABC and urge the network to reschedule the series to a weeknight. Beginning March 28, *Twin Peaks* returned to its original Thursday night time slot before the network put it on a second hiatus four weeks later. Fans formed a group called the "Coalition Opposed to Offing Peaks," or "COOP," and sent over ten thousand letters to ABC in an attempt to save the series. The last two episodes of the second season aired back-to-back on Sunday, June 10, after the network announced its cancellation (Lavery 1–3).

Almost as legendary as *Twin Peaks* itself is the fandom it has inspired.[5] Viewing parties gathered in 1990 to watch episodes and consume cherry pie, a trend that prompted the Du-par's chain to sell whole, fresh-baked cherry pies at a discounted price (Ochoa 9), bringing *Twin Peaks* full circle to the alleged place of its inception. Nationwide fan discussions transpired at alt.tv.twinpeaks on the electronic bulletin board Usenet. In 1992, John Thorne and Craig Miller's fanzine *Wrapped in Plastic* began its thirteen-year publication, and in 1993, Snoqualmie, North Bend, and Fall City hosted the first fan-organized *Twin Peaks* Festival (an event held annually to

5

date). The series gained an unprecedentedly huge following in Japan, where fans attended mock funerals for Laura and took group tours to the shooting locations, donning plastic sheets in deference to their beloved character (Pollack 18).

From 2011 to 2015, Frost and Lynch worked on the script for *The Return*, and when they announced its production in October of 2014, *Peaks* fandom returned in a renaissance of activity. The series has been nominated for a total of twenty-three Primetime Emmy Awards and won only two, suggesting its appeal is still primarily subcultural rather than industrial. Outlets such as *Blue Rose Magazine*, the website welcometotwinpeaks .com, and a variety of social media accounts have continued the tradition of fanzine publication and online discussion to support an interactive fan community. Many contemporary fans comprise a new generation of viewers introduced to *Twin Peaks* on DVD, Blu-ray, and streaming services, including podcasters, artists, musicians, and even burlesque performers. As evidenced by the #SaveTwinPeaks viral media campaign, *Twin Peaks* fans also overlap with fans of Lynch as a film auteur. Feeling that the production budget and number of episodes were inadequate for what he envisioned, he pulled out of *The Return* in 2015, but to the relief of campaigning fans, Showtime eventually agreed to his terms and he came back to the project roughly a month later. The 140-day shoot for *The Return* began in September of 2015 (Lynch and McKenna 475–78), and it aired from May through September of 2017. Interpretations of its story, theories about its mythology, debates over its politics, and evaluations of its quality have not ceased. To date, neither Frost nor Lynch has confirmed more *Twin Peaks*, but it is clear that their "soap noir," as the *New York Times* dubbed it, is here to stay (Gerard C22).

Entering the Study of *Twin Peaks*

Perhaps one of the underacknowledged elements of *Twin Peaks* as a television milestone is not only its status as a distinctive cultural product but also how it engages in conversation about culture, often by the multiple shapes it takes in the culture of US media. While psychoanalysis has been a prominent theoretical framework in the study of David Lynch's films, represented preeminently by Todd McGowan's *The Impossible David Lynch*, our project is neither strictly auteurist nor exclusively intended for a specialized academic readership. Hopefully of equal interest to scholars and fans alike, this book remains dedicated to the primary texts themselves in their cultural contexts. One aim of writing this monograph has been to create space for appreciating *Twin Peaks*'s own critical project. Far from a nostalgic celebration of the small-town idyll, *Twin Peaks* and *The Return* explore the underside of familiar tropes of community and small-town life within the landscape of American culture and history. Mark Frost cites Odysseus in his description of *The Return* (O'Falt), inflecting Cooper's travels with Homer's theme of *nostos*, or going home.

But the journeys of characters in *Twin Peaks* reflect a more complicated trajectory, activated by a "homesickness" in which one finds sickness within the home: depredation and toxicity at the very center of the hearth. The fire that walks with the characters and events within *Twin Peaks* serves as a bad twin of the homey hearth imagined by American myths of domesticity. This fire doesn't warm its bystanders but painfully burns away their badges of normalcy and the veneer of routine. For all its moments of humor, strange details, and earnest depiction of friendship, *Twin Peaks* offers a deeply affecting meditation on the violation of and within the home and the lack of fulfillment for those who search there for consolation. As a site of incest, violence, and horrible trauma, Laura Palmer's home is no place of comfort. Further, as Lindsay Hallam observes, *Twin Peaks* reveals the fissures in a community that has to some extent repressed the violence and horrors that have beset it, refusing to own "the wider collective guilt that must be borne by Twin Peaks and its residents" (*Twin Peaks* 111).

This book focuses attention on *Twin Peaks*'s serious contemplation of the challenges facing individuals who wish to connect amidst the "noises" of institutionalized social forms and the potentially violent disruptions of ego, with masculine power posing a particularly virulent threat to safety and happiness. As many are aware, Lynch's work has generated some controversy in his representation of women (see, for example, George, Lafky, and Ramsay). But *Twin Peaks* doesn't endorse or exploit the violence it depicts; its episodes and paratexts represent the struggles of individuals, especially women, to find release from pain, oppression, and physical or psychological imprisonments.

We see *Twin Peaks* as deeply empathic and revelatory regarding the plight of women, the depiction of Laura in particular registering the strength and power of a woman fighting (over decades and across time and space continuums) against both masculine forces and the stereotypes about women and society that further entrap her and other women in *Twin Peaks*. Indeed, Hallam sees in Lynch's feature film prequel *Twin Peaks: Fire Walk with Me* (1992) "a testament of [Laura's] strength" (*Twin Peaks* 20). Rather than focusing on the "stilled image" of Laura, "Homecoming Queen," victim of Leland/BOB's incest-rape and murder, Hallam shifts viewers' perspective to Laura's resistance to becoming possessed by evil: "Laura steadfastly refused to surrender. This is not the story of how she came to die, but rather the story that reveals how Laura is in fact the strongest of them all" (21).

Laura's dynamism, embodied by the remarkable performance of Sheryl Lee, energizes the worlds of *Twin Peaks*, promoting not only the values of empathy and creativity but also an ethos more generally that stands against multiple forms of objectification and reification. *Twin Peaks* is a world-building phenomenon traversing different textual worlds across media. Our book argues that as a transmedia phenomenon, the series resists and often critiques categories that impose narrow meanings on culture. We contend that the series problematizes the cultural functions of art and medium, genre, identity, and indeed textuality itself. Following Agent Cooper's advice to "hear" and "see the other side," *Twin Peaks* teaches us how to work as social agents outside of the definitions and categorization that so often govern our ways of knowing and being in the material world.

As the subsequent chapters investigate, *Twin Peaks* expands and blurs socially constructed boundaries in common binaries such as high art vs. popular culture; cinema vs. television; authorship vs. collaboration; one genre vs. another; "good" vs. "bad" women; organically coherent vs. fragmented subjectivities; and texts vs. paratexts. Chapter 1 looks at publicity and critical discourses on authorship that framed the series as an auteurist project akin to art cinema rather than a prime-time soap opera. Yet, the collaboration between Lynch and Frost in the context of television production challenges notions of medium specificity. Despite the way critics sought to distance the series from the soap opera as a popular genre, Chapter 2 explores both melodrama and noir as elastic generic sources for *Twin Peaks* that need not presume a postmodern stance. Chapters 3 and 4 suggest that performance in *Twin Peaks*— whether the social role-playing of the femme fatale or the acting of the series' cast members—speaks to a conception of the self as multiple and performative rather than "naturally" fixed or singular. The boundaries in *Twin Peaks* expand further, as Chapter 5 explains, when accounting for the rich transmedia story achieved through adaptation and remediation in the paratextual life of the series. An overriding principle guiding these creative expansions is an affirmation of human agency despite our common struggles to be good "agents" in a world that's weirder than we sometimes think it is.

Behind the Red Curtains

Questions of Authorship

One of the ways *Twin Peaks* arrived on the television land-scape of the early 1990s was under the banner of cocre-ators and executive producers Mark Frost and David Lynch. Frost was a three-year staff writer for the groundbreaking ensemble police drama *Hill Street Blues* (NBC, 1981–87) and Lynch was the Academy Award–nominated film director of *The Elephant Man* (1980) and *Blue Velvet* (1986). The latter film ignited controversy for its depiction of sadomasochistic sex and violence, but it also ushered Lynch into more main-stream attention and turned a modest profit. Over a decade earlier, his experimental first feature *Eraserhead* (1977) had endeared him to the Greenwich Village "underground movie" crowd, who gave the film a cult following during the course of its midnight runs at the Cinema Village (from the fall of 1977 to the summer of 1978) and the Waverly Theater, now the IFC Center (from the summer of 1979 to mid-September of 1981) (Hoberman and Rosenbaum 220). This chapter looks at the way inter- and extratextual sources constructed *Twin Peaks* as a "Lynchian" text notwithstanding the inherently collaborative nature of television authorship. Out of the twenty-nine total, Frost directed one episode and contributed to ten scripts, while

Lynch directed five episodes with a hand in three scripts, in addition to the pilot, which he directed and cowrote with Frost (see Appendix).

ABC was able to take advantage of Frost's reputation in the industry and especially Lynch's critical acceptance as an auteur. The day the pilot aired, the *New York Times* ran a publicity story with the ready-made headline "When *Blue Velvet* Meets *Hill Street Blues*" (Woodward, "When *Blue Velvet*" 31). Framed by a discourse on authorship, the reception conditions of *Twin Peaks* allowed for a reading strategy through which audiences could identify the series as a new television crime drama—both innovative and provocative—with the cultural capital of art house cinema. *Entertainment Weekly*'s April 6, 1990, cover featured not cast members but Lynch himself, leaning on a canted television set that displayed an extreme close-up of an eyeball, presumably belonging to Laura Palmer. The television set both draws attention to his transmedia authorship and links him to the diegesis of the pilot (recall that when Cooper plays a videotape of Laura and the camcorder zooms in on her face, he sees a clue reflected in an extreme close-up of her eye). At this point, Lynch was more visible than ever, and the headline spoke to the recognizability of his pop surrealist style: "David Lynch Brings His Bizarre Vision to Prime Time: The Year's Best Show!" The cover story provided a textbook overview of his directorial signatures (see Jerome), while the rest of the issue included four additional articles on the production of the series, along with an "A+" review (see Tucker). Wearing a slightly oversized black suit jacket and white dress shirt, buttoned to the top, with his brown hair coifed into a messy pompadour, Lynch also had a signature look.

Like Alfred Hitchcock, he is a playful illusionist and an audience manipulator associated with "thrilling" sensation, who made use of both cinema and television and worked across both sides of the camera. Not only did he appear in promotional and publicity material such as the *Entertainment Weekly*

David Lynch as Gordon Cole (*Twin Peaks*, Episode 25).

cover but he also guest starred on the series as FBI regional bureau chief Gordon Cole (introduced over speaker phone in Episode 4 and in person in Episode 13). Motivated by Gordon's acute hearing loss, Lynch amplified his voice in his performance of the character such that his manner of speaking—the flat northwestern US accent, halting rhythm, and nasal, almost high-pitched tone—remains as unmistakable as his fashion. Lynch's image served a similar function to that of Hitchcock, who also donned a particular uniform (white shirt, black suit, and black tie). Creating the "idea" of Hitchcock through his personality and physical appearance, the droll, heavyset host of his named anthology series suggested an overriding authorial presence despite his collaborative involvement in production with inconsistent degrees of authorial control (Kapsis 31–32). If Lynch is an auteur, a title he most certainly deserves, he is also a celebrity-director, and the two roles shaped each other in the production and reception history of *Twin Peaks*.[6]

Journalists who interviewed Lynch seemed to relish in the apparent incongruity between the horrific content they had witnessed in his films and the earnest, mild-mannered person they met: a self-identified Eagle Scout from suburban Idaho who claimed not to watch television (Shales C8) and to get ideas over coffee and milkshakes at Bob's Big Boy (Weinstein N8; Woodward, "Dark Lens" 21; Zoglin, "Like Nothing" 97). He expressed a fascination with industrial spaces such as factories and machine rooms, an admiration for painters Edward Hopper and Francis Bacon, and an indebtedness to the writing of Franz Kafka, but communicates in youthful 1950s slang ("oh boy," "pretty cool," and "Holy smokes!" were among the quoted Lynch-isms) (Shales C8). In short, he personified the very tensions that fascinated critics in *Blue Velvet*—darkness and light, weird and ordinary, hip and square. The executive producer of *The Elephant Man*, Stuart Cornfeld, once called him "Jimmy Stewart from Mars," a quote commonly attributed to Mel Brooks, whose company produced the film (Rodley xii), but regardless of its origin, it may as well have been brand Lynch. And the term "Lynchian" was about to become a household adjective, what author David Foster Wallace famously defined as "a particular kind of irony where the very macabre and the very mundane combine in such a way as to reveal the former's perpetual containment within the latter" (161).

In the months leading up to the pilot, story after story generated buzz by trying to articulate that ineffable Lynchian sensibility as an authorial context for the series. For the *Los Angeles Times*, *Twin Peaks* was "[a] serialized murder mystery that is all mood—one moment the height of campiness, the next disturbingly eerie" (Weinstein N8). The *New York Times Magazine* put Lynch on the cover and compared him to European surrealists Luis Buñuel and Jean Cocteau, remarking that his "taste in risky, often grotesque material has made him, perhaps, Hollywood's most revered eccentric, sort of a psychopathic Norman Rock-well" (Woodward, "Dark Lens" 20). *Rolling Stone* detailed Lynch's meticulous preparation and handiwork, such as creating BOB's unholy alter for the United Kingdom home video version of the pilot by assembling found objects on a mound of dirt with candles he brought personally (Pond 51, 53). On the other hand, the author notes how Lynch improvised on the shoot, intuitively seizing upon accidents or problems, such as allowing a broken light to flicker to achieve a certain atmosphere in another scene (electrical flickers, of course, turned into a visual motif in the series) (120). As the *Washington Post* affirmed, Lynch had made some "spookily mercurial" films and with *Twin Peaks* was "reinventing the prime-time soap opera" (Shales C1). The day after the pilot aired, *Time* echoed this growing consensus by comparing the cliffhanger question-cum-marketing catchphrase of the series—"Who Killed Laura Palmer?"—to the one for *Dallas* (CBS, 1978–91), the prime-time soap opera par excellence: "At worst, *Twin Peaks* could turn into an aesthete's version of 'Who Shot J. R.?' At best, it will be mesmerizing" (Zoglin, "Like Nothing" 97). *Time's* interview with Lynch reinforced an auteurist rationale for the distinctiveness of *Twin Peaks*, which, the author proselytized, is "like nothing you've ever seen in prime time—or on God's earth. It may be the most hauntingly original work ever done for TV" (96).

An auteurist reading is hardly unthinkable. Fans of Lynch would have noticed connections between *Twin Peaks* and *Blue Velvet* through their story lines (mystery, sex crimes, and drug trade in a deceptively wholesome lumber town), characters (quirky detectives played by Kyle MacLachlan), music (a jazz-inflected score by Angelo Badalamenti and songs by synth pop balladeer Julee Cruise), and retro teenage dream worlds. One journalist pointed out that *Blue Velvet* ends where the title sequence of *Twin Peaks* begins, on a shot of a robin in a tree (Woodward, "Dark Lens" 43), although the bird is actually a Bewick's wren. What makes this auteurist reception atypical for a series in the early 1990s is that television "auteurs" were historically understood as writers and executive producers ("showrunners," in the parlance of twenty-first-century television discourse), whereas directors vary from episode to episode and therefore a single director may not exert a consistent creative force behind a series as a whole (see Abbott; Hallam, "May the Giant").

Born in 1946 in Missoula, Montana, Lynch moved around the northwestern US during the early years of his life. The Lynch family first relocated to Sandpoint, Idaho, when he was two months old, then to Spokane, Washington, in 1949, and finally to Boise, Idaho, in 1955 (they spent 1954 in Durham, North Carolina, where Lynch's father, a research scientist for the US Department of Agriculture, completed his doctorate in forestry at Duke University). It was in Alexandria, Virginia, riding out his disenchanted high-school years, where he fell in love with painting. After aborted attempts to study at the School of the Museum of Fine Arts at Tufts in Boston and the Salzburg International Summer Academy of Fine Arts in Austria, he enrolled at the Pennsylvania Academy of Fine Arts in Philadelphia. Lynch's time in Philadelphia introduced him to making films, including a stop-motion animated short projected onto a sculpted screen called *Six Men Getting Sick (Six Times)* (1967) and, after he left the academy, a short that combined live action with animation called *The Alphabet* (1968). Filmmaking helped him to realize his desire to create a "painting that would really be able to move" (Rodley 37). A production grant from the newly established American Film Institute (AFI) funded a short called *The Grandmother* (1970), which led to Lynch's decisive move to Los Angeles later that year with his first wife, Peggy Lentz, and their daughter Jennifer. There, he started a fellowship at the AFI Center for Advanced Film Studies (now the AFI Conservatory) and from 1971 to 1976 labored intermittently on *Eraserhead*. Jennifer Lynch would go on to write *The Secret Diary of Laura Palmer* (1990) (see Chapter 5).

Seven years his junior, Frost was born in 1953 in New York City, grew up in Los Angeles and Minneapolis, and (coincidentally) also learned his craft in Pennsylvania, where he studied acting, directing, and playwriting at Carnegie Mellon University. After cutting his teeth in Hollywood as a television writer on *The Six Million Dollar Man* (ABC, 1974–78), he joined the writing staff of *Hill Street Blues*. Frost's other writing credits include episodes of *The Equalizer* (CBS, 1985–89) and the occult horror film *The Believers* (1987), directed by John Schlesinger, but his work on *Hill Street Blues* built his reputation in the 1980s, earning a Primetime Emmy Award nomination and Writers Guild of America Award for Episode 14 from Season 4, "Grace Under Pressure" (originally aired on February 2, 1984). Two members of his family left their marks on the *Twin Peaks* universe. Scott Frost, his brother, wrote Episodes 15 and 21, as well as the tie-in novel *The Autobiography of F.B.I. Special Agent Dale Cooper: My Life, My Tapes* (1991) and audiobook *"Diane . . .": The Twin Peaks Tapes of Agent Cooper* (see Chapter 5). Actor Warren Frost, their late father, played "Doc" Will Hayward.

In 1989, Lynch and Frost founded Lynch/Frost Productions to produce the series. Gary Levine, the vice president for dramatic series development at ABC, said the network wanted "to attract both Lynch devotees and soap opera fans," explaining that although Lynch's deliberate pace as a filmmaker was "unsuitable for most commercial broadcasts," Frost "understands how to work within an extended story with lots of characters" (Woodward, "When *Blue Velvet*" 31). The press amply covered Lynch's biography and background in painting, characterizing him as the visual artist who set the tone of *Twin Peaks* and Frost as the writer with the television know-how. According to a *Newsweek* interview, "Lynch thinks like a painter, not like a writer: he never talks about themes and messages; what interests him are textures, moods, contrasts, silences. 'When you can talk about it,' Lynch says, 'you're not using cinema'" (Ansen 68). The *Village Voice* practically offered an introduction to mise-en-scène analysis as a prologue to its interview, illustrating how *Twin Peaks* differed from traditional television in terms of Lynch's uniquely cinematic style (see Taubin). Yet, in spite of his almost "pure cinema" approach, he admitted that Frost taught him how to organize visual story-telling around eleven-minute dramatic "acts" to accommodate for commercial breaks (the pilot aired with only five breaks, as opposed to the conventional seven) (Woodward, "When 'Blue Velvet'" 31; Jerome 38, 40).

Between May and December of 1990, the *Twin Peaks* media blitz continued in full force. Cast members rotated in the guest seat on *Late Night with David Letterman* and graced the covers of entertainment and lifestyle magazines including *Entertainment Weekly*, *US*, *Esquire*, *TV Guide*, *Rolling Stone*, *GQ*, and *Playboy*. Frost accompanied Peggy Lipton, Piper Laurie, Dana Ashbrook, Mädchen Amick, Eric DaRe, and Sheryl Lee on the *Phil Donahue Show* (WNBC, 1985–96) to inform audiences that a second season had been renewed, and the night before its premiere, Kyle MacLachlan hosted *Saturday Night Live* (NBC, 1975-present) and poked fun at his Cooper character in an affectionate par-ody skit. Articles in *New York*, *Newsweek*, and *Time* assessed the popularity and possible future of the series (see Leonard; Leerhsen with White; and Zoglin, "A Sleeper"), while *TV Guide* asked four different authors to solve the Laura Palmer case (see Elm). Magazines as disparate as *Rolling Stone* and the *National Review* profiled Lynch (see Breskin; Sobran), but it was the *Time* cover story on October 1, 1990, that announced the "Czar of Bizarre" as a newsworthy interview subject (see Corliss). To be sure, 1990 was Lynch's year: the N. No. N. Gallery in Dallas, Texas, and the Tavelli Gallery in Aspen, Colorado, exhibited his art, and his Southern Gothic road film *Wild at Heart* won the Palme d'Or, the top prize at the Cannes International Film Festival.

Twin Peaks was not his only foray outside of painting and cinema. As a photographer, he captured industrial images and created "kits," or arrangements of labeled animal parts. From 1983 to 1992, he wrote and drew the absurdist comic strip *The Angriest Dog in the World*, which circulated in the *L. A. Reader* and the *L. A. Weekly*. In 1988, he directed a creepy, anti-littering public service announcement for the New York Department of Sanitation, a commercial for Yves St. Laurent's women's perfume *Opium*, and four commercials for the Calvin Klein men's perfume *Obsession* (*Twin Peaks* cast members James Marshall, Lara Flynn Boyle, and Heather Graham starred in three). With Badalamenti, he coproduced Cruise's 1989 album *Floating into the Night* (Lynch wrote the lyrics for all ten songs). Half of the songs are heard in *Twin Peaks*, including an instrumental version of the lead single "Falling," the theme song for the series. On November 10, 1989, he directed a performance piece for the Brooklyn Academy of Music titled *Industrial Symphony No. 1: The Dream of the Brokenhearted* inspired by Nicolas Cage and Laura Dern's romantic outlaw couple from *Wild at Heart*, which featured music by Badalamenti and Cruise (Michael J. Anderson, the Man from Another Place in *Twin Peaks*, played a woodsman). Lynch even directed an alternate music video for Chris Isaak's hit song "Wicked Game" that *Wild at Heart* popularized.

More than any of these projects, though, Lynch's relationship to the art world and art cinema gave *Twin Peaks* a prestige factor and brought a level of experimentation that places it in the category of "art television," or "a sort of television comparable to art films," as defined by film historian Kristin Thompson (108). Following the likes of Michael Mann and Steven Spielberg, Lynch was not the first director to move between film and television on a US network, but he was the first art cinema auteur to do so with commercial success. Building from earlier scholarship on this mode of film practice (see Bordwell), Thompson reminds us that art cinema straddles a middle-ground style and market between the mainstream and the avant-garde, the latter of which usually consists of non-narrative films exhibited in museums, campus environments, and filmmaking coopera- tives. Whereas classical narrative adheres to causality, closure, and spaciotemporal continuity, art films loosen that storytelling logic and may altogether violate its clarity. Art cinema empha- sizes ambiguity and psychological or quotidian realism. The auteur often makes him- or herself known as a formal element in the art film, suggesting that what the film "says" derives from an artist's personal vision and expression (Kristin Thompson 110–15). *Twin Peaks* serves as an exemplary case study for art television, an auteur-driven series with geographically indeter- minate settings (the White and Black Lodges, the Red Room), dream states that blur with reality, narrative digressions, epi- sodic and open-ended plotlines, obscure symbolism, and stylistic excesses. Cooper was not the classical, goal-oriented protagonist in his pursuit of Laura's murderer, but a "protago- nist pursuing what threatens to be an ever-receding goal" (133).

Television historian Robert J. Thompson posits a similar ar- gument about *Twin Peaks* as an example of "Quality TV," but he situates so-called quality programming within larger changes in television itself. The term "Quality TV" gained currency in pop- ular and industrial discourse by the early 1980s with the debut of *Hill Street Blues* (12). Rather than speaking to an aesthetic judgment, the term refers more to a generic style of prime- time, hour-long network dramas that lasted up to the 1993–94 season. In addition to Lynch's artistic pedigree, *Twin Peaks* fits every criterion of "quality" Thompson outlines: an unconven- tional style; generic hybridity and revisionism (see Chapter 2); complex writing with character development and narrative continuity from episode to episode; a large ensemble cast; re- alistic or controversial subject matter (in this case, incest, mur- der, drugs, and prostitution); an urban, upscale, well-educated demographic; critical acclaim and award attention; and extra- textual battles with a profit-minded network and nonapprecia- tive audience that suggest a commitment to art over commerce (13–16). ABC, in particular, had made an investment in edgier,

19

more daring programming since the 1980s in an attempt to rebrand its corporate identity and recoup the losses in network television's dwindling audience (152–53).

Both Kristin Thompson's and Robert J. Thompson's accounts provide important contexts for the historical significance of *Twin Peaks*. Lynch collaborated with Frost to create a television drama consistent with his signature style and personal vision as an art cinema auteur; they even launched it with a four-million-dollar, two-hour pilot, conceived as a film and shot on location, which the network aired on the *ABC Sunday Night Movie* (Jerome 40; Lynch and McKenna 273). The subsequent Lynch-directed episodes were crucial anchors for the series: Episode 2 (the introduction of the Red Room); Episode 8 (the two-hour Season 2 premiere, another *ABC Sunday Night Movie*); Episode 9 (the development of BOB's role in Laura's murder); Episode 14 (Leland's identification as BOB's human host); and Episode 29 (the Season 2 finale, aired back-to-back with Episode 28 on the *ABC Monday Night Movie*). Rising television and independent film directors, editors, and cinematographers came on board to direct other episodes, and although they were able to bring their own sensibilities to the series, they were held responsible for maintaining a general fidelity to the blueprint Lynch and Frost established in the pilot (Abbott 179–82). The series was shot on 35mm and edited on film, each episode averaging one million dollars in production cost, but at the time Lynch disapproved of television's aspect ratio and sound-image quality as compared to cinema (Rodley 175–76). Few censorship regulations hemmed in the writers and directors, and Lynch essentially retained final cut on the pilot (Jerome 42; Rodley 177–78).

Lynch's film sensibility, however, did not by itself reinvent network television and revolutionize the quality of the medium. Rather, as Robert J. Thompson recounts, he found an initial (if unlikely) compatibility with new directions in the industry that had been in development over the previous decade. What is more, the attribution Lynch received as the auteur behind *Twin Peaks* served to enhance the cultural value of the series and of television more broadly (see Abbott; Hallam, "May the Giant"). Television of the twenty-first century has seen a generation of film directors working in similar capacities, with a greater public and critical appreciation of television authorship and aesthetics.

The collaborative relationship between Lynch and Frost was not without friction during the first two seasons. After the pilot wrapped and as ABC deliberated about picking up the series, Lynch moved on to shoot *Wild at Heart* in the summer of 1989, leaving Frost at the helm of the first season once the network ordered the next seven episodes. Frost reportedly grew frustrated with the assumption that *Twin Peaks* was primarily Lynch's series, having cowritten the pilot and the first two episodes with him, then assembling a writing staff that included Harley Peyton and Robert Engels (Hughes 107; Lynch and McKenna 256, 260). While Lynch adamantly wanted to defer solving the murder mystery, allowing it to recede to the background as other related story lines came into focus (Rodley 180), Frost preferred more clarity and closure (Hughes 107). Nobody in the cast knew the identity of Laura's murderer. Cast members started receiving the script with their scenes alone to ensure secrecy around the story ("Secrets").

ABC finally pressured them to identify who killed Laura Palmer and they complied in Episode 14, just before the series lost authorial coherence (Hughes 107). Initially, when other writers contributed to the series, Frost and Lynch gave them ground rules and story lines to follow, and even recorded their meetings for the writers' reference to ensure consistency with the narrative and tone they envisioned (Lynch and McKenna 256; Rodley 174–75). By the second season, Lynch was not in agreement with all of the new story lines, some of which he had not preapproved (Lynch and McKenna 260), and after Episode 14 he more or less removed himself from any substantive authorial role until directing Episode 29, which he largely reconceived from its original script (Hughes 107; Rodley 182). After Episode 16, when Leland dies and BOB escapes, Frost did not directly contribute to the writing of any scripts until Episode 26. "There were certainly some weaknesses in the second season," reflected Frost, who felt he and Lynch were "stretched too thin" with other commitments, including Frost's first feature film as a director, *Storyville* (1992), which he cowrote with Lee Reynolds (Lynch and McKenna 259). From Lynch's perspective, there were too many other writers and directors whose vision of *Twin Peaks* he did not recognize as his and Frost's own (Lynch and McKenna 277; Rodley 182).

Lynch/Frost Productions struggled with other television ventures in the early 1990s. In the midst of *Twin Peaks*, Frost created *American Chronicles* (Fox, 1990), a documentary anthology series about unusual social customs in the US, but it was canceled after three months. Following the cancellation of *Twin Peaks*, he and Lynch cocreated *On the Air* (ABC, 1992), a slapstick sitcom about a dysfunctional 1950s variety show. *On the Air* was canceled in the US after the broadcast of only three episodes (a total of seven were shot and shown in Europe).

When the time came to revisit *Twin Peaks* twenty-five years later, Lynch's reputation as a film auteur had survived a lost television audience and a scathing reception of *Twin Peaks: Fire Walk with Me* (see Chapter 5). His quintessentially Lynchian film *Mulholland Drive* (2001) earned him a Best Director Award at Cannes, an Academy Award nomination, and critical acclaim that has only grown over the years; at one point, he allegedly considered making the film as a pilot for a *Twin Peaks* spin-off about Audrey Horne in Hollywood (Lynch and McKenna 363, 383). Now, he was excited by what cable television could offer him as a director—the possibilities for a "continuing story"— and he heralded cable as "the new art-house" (Smith).

To that end, he approached *The Return* as a long-form film for which premium cable television was the only possible exhibition venue, unencumbered by commercial interruptions and censorship restrictions. Reuniting with Frost, he cofounded a production company called Rancho Rosa Partnership, named after the Las Vegas housing development depicted in *The Return*, and cowrote a complete script of over four hundred pages, with no episode divisions. MacLachlan was allowed exclusive access to read the entire script, while the rest of the cast members received only their individual lines (Lynch and McKenna 479). Putting to rest concerns from fans and critics over the authenticity of *The Return*, Lynch would direct the entire project for Showtime, whose parent company owns the *Twin Peaks* distribution rights and where old ally Gary Levine was president of programming (Jensen 29; Ryan, "Peak Performance" 44). The series was shot with a feature film crew on digital cameras in multiple cities over a span of 142 days (Jensen 29; Lynch and McKenna 476). Showtime aired *The Return* in hour-long "parts," eighteen in all, as Lynch insisted they should not be viewed as discrete episodes within a series (Jensen 29). In fact, it was never officially referred to in television lexicon as a third "season."

Once again, *Twin Peaks* was back in the media spotlight and, with his greater authorial freedom and control, Lynch took center stage. Cover stories ran in the premier European cinephile magazines *Cahiers du Cinéma* (the origin of *la politique des auteurs*) and *Sight & Sound*, as well as in more familiar places such as *TV Guide* and *Entertainment Weekly*, the latter of which published three variant covers for a special *Twin Peaks* preview issue. The flagship trade journal *Variety* published a cover story that featured photos of and interviews with Lynch, MacLachlan, and Laura Dern, MacLachlan's *Blue Velvet* costar who joined the cast of *The Return* (see Ryan, "Peak Performance"). After all, Lynch was as much a star as either of them or any of the 217 actors, for that matter, reprising both his role as director and his character Gordon Cole, now deputy director of the FBI. MacLachlan and Lynch were among 27 actors who reprised their roles from the first two seasons.

Following Lynch's reading strategy, some critics included *The Return* on their lists of the ten best "films" of 2017, and it even ranked in first and second place for *Cahiers du Cinéma* and *Sight & Sound*, respectively. A spirited and ultimately fruitless debate raged—mostly between film and television buffs over online social networks—as to the rightful media jurisdiction of *The Return*. Of course, like the original *Twin Peaks*, *The Return* is a television program, but at the risk of deterministic or overly literal thinking, its exhibition origin should not preclude it from *also* being appreciated as a film, like *Twin Peaks: Fire Walk with Me* (Parts 1 and 2 screened at Cannes, where a five-minute standing ovation ensued, and all eighteen parts played over three nights at the Museum of Modern Art). What is exciting about *The Return* is not that it represents postmillennial television at its best or redeems the medium through cinematic auteurism but that it shows how the *Twin Peaks* universe continues to exist at the threshold of multiple, mutable worlds (diegetic, generic, textual, temporal, and technological). The mixed-media art of *Twin Peaks* need not be defined according to where or how one views it. Instead, it defies the very viewing conventions one expects from it, be they televisual, cinematic, or otherwise.

Reading Maps, Plotting Coordinates

Genre and Intertextuality

Of all the media outlets that publicized David Lynch's author- ship during the first year of *Twin Peaks*, perhaps one of the most surprising was *Soap Opera Weekly*, which featured him on the cover of its October 16, 1990, issue. Clearly, both author- ship and genre served as organizing systems for the publicity and reception of the series (between 1991 and 1992, it was also nominated for a total of fourteen *Soap Opera Digest* Awards). The soap-opera genre arouses what Ien Ang calls a "tragic structure of feeling," which is "made possible by the way in which the soap opera text is formally and ideologically structured," and therefore can fall under the umbrella category of melodrama, a cultural form "whose main effect is the stirring up of the emotions" (61). Melodrama has long been synonymous with "failed tragedy," denigrated as a sensationalistic drama for popular audiences that plays on public emotions instead of appealing to the intellect; trades in flat characters, banal stories, and clichés; and stretches narrative credibility to the point of appearing ridiculous (62). The classist associations between and among soap opera, melo- drama, and "inferior culture" (62) would seem to render *Twin Peaks* incompatible with the highbrow reading strategies identi- fied in the previous chapter.

One of the ways critics attempted to mitigate this problem of taste politics was by making claims to a hip, ironic distance—a mocking or "Lynching" of the genre, if you will. When informed that *Twin Peaks* was being read as a soap opera send-up, Lynch reportedly "bristled" and told *TV Guide*, "Soap operas to me should not be camp. These are very real characters," adding that they "feel and do what they do with all their heart" (Carlson 22). He maintained that "putting yourself above something else" and "poking fun" at it is "not creative," but "a lower kind of humor" (22). Television packaging agent Tony Krantz, who represented Lynch and Mark Frost at Creative Artists Agency, showed them the 1957 Hollywood melodrama *Peyton Place*, an adaptation of the scandalous bestseller by Grace Metalious published the previous year, as a way to help them shape their ideas before pitching the series to ABC. Although Lynch was not a fan of the film (Lynch and McKenna 247), he used to watch soap operas, and the novel also inspired the first high-profile, star-driven soap opera to air on prime-time network television in the US, which ran on ABC from 1964 to 1969 (Linda Ruth Williams 47). In fact, Lynch saw the soap-opera format as a potentially more accommodating venue than feature films to write an immersive, continuing story with multiple characters that could unfold in a specific location, providing him with opportunities as a director to concentrate on the emotionalism and idiosyncrasies of performance (Rodley 155–56).[7]

Twin Peaks is not only a soap opera but also qualifies as a police procedural and mystery series that might situate it under the category of noir as much as melodrama, apropos of Lynch's neo-noir *Blue Velvet*, commonly invoked as a companion text.[8] Academics have theorized its generic hybridity and allusiveness as symptoms of its postmodernism, reading the series as a subversive noir parody (see Richardson), an exercise in empty formal play and politically regressive "fun" (see Ramsay), and an eclectic bricolage that activates both progressive and reactionary readings, ironic distance, and sincere empathy (see Collins).[9] However, we are interested in a more precise understanding of its genre conventions and how they function. We argue that by operating in the broad categories of melodrama and noir, *Twin Peaks* exploits the already multigeneric registers of film and television storytelling that allow for textual variability and intertextual signifying practices. Exhausting the multigeneric qualities of *Twin Peaks* is beyond the scope of this short volume, but other scholars have analyzed the series in relation to science fiction (see Telotte), horror (see Jowett and Abbott), and the US frontier myth (see Carroll).[10] By limiting our focus to melodrama and noir, we are merely privileging its dominant generic identities as a soap opera and murder mystery in accord with the way advertising and the popular press labeled the series for audiences.

Generic Labels and Definitions

Postmodernist readings presume a certain stability of genres in media and popular culture, which have been neither pure and discrete nor static and fixed as systems of classification in the production or reception of a text. As Barry Keith Grant reminds us, "genre movies have always been hybrid, combinative in practice" (23). For example, the canonical Hollywood western *Stagecoach* (1939) was promoted as a "*Grand Hotel* [1932] on wheels," and it also shares a kinship with the road film and the disaster film (Grant 23–24). Moreover, the necessary repetitions and differences in a genre make it possible for change, self-conscious revision and self-parody, and even reaffirmation or transformation over time, "with each new film and cycle adding to the tradition and modifying it" (35). Genres are dynamic, ongoing processes, as generic phases overlap and fall in and out of fashion (34–39). *Twin Peaks* certainly intensifies the juxtaposition of tones and conventions achieved through its generic heterogeneity, alternating between sadness and humor or humor and horror, for example. Yet, we view the series less as an example of postmodern media and its shifting subject positions than as a self-conscious extension of film and television's standard business of genre mixing, illustrating just how flexible and porous genres can be (and have been).

Contemporary television may even accelerate a genre's transformation faster than cinema. Genres structurally regulate repetition and difference among texts, and between text and audience (White 46). Mimi White contends that borrowing popular, existing forms and combining them into new configurations satisfies the demand to fill a large number of programming slots and maintain a wide viewership over a continuous, regular flow of programming (46). This absence of generic unity or consistency suggests that "no single genre can adequately account for the narrative and dramatic practices of the show as a whole" (43), but programs may still retain narrative and dramatic coherence. Blurring the lines between familiar genres has been "the basis for realist textuality," as in *Hill Street Blues*, and "shifts in generic register remain identifiable" (43).

Rather than as a product of postmodernism, *Twin Peaks* might be understood more historically within the aesthetic norms of the prime-time soap opera that began in the 1980s, of which *Hill Street Blues* was a formative part. Jason Mittell locates *Twin Peaks* at the vanguard of narrative complexity in 1990s television, but cites programs such as *Dallas*, *Dynasty* (ABC, 1981–89), and *St. Elsewhere* (NBC, 1982–88) as important precursors with their "episodic plotlines alongside multiepisode arcs and ongoing relationship dramas" (Mittell 32). *Twin Peaks* "expanded the role of story arcs across episodes and seasons" (33) that characterized soaps of the previous decade, while new technologies such as the VCR and the Internet supported an even greater degree of narrative complexity. Audiences could now record and rewatch episodes, catch up on what they missed, and discuss the series with fellow fans online (31–32). At the time of its original airing, *Twin Peaks* was reportedly the most videotaped series on television (Lavery, "Introduction" 11).

Turning to genre does not diminish Frost and Lynch's contributions as television auteurs. To the contrary, as Grant points out, a genre gives an artist a "flexible tradition within which to work," and many of the major auteurs in the Hollywood studio system "developed their vision within particular genres, such as Samuel Fuller with the war film, John Ford with the western and Douglas Sirk with the melodrama" (Grant 56). But looking to Frost and Lynch themselves for validation may not yield helpful results. Determining the nature of Lynch's directorial influences or frameworks seems nearly impossible; he shuns questions of intentionality and never offers ideological or interpretative explanations of his work (Rodley 27–28, 63–64). Whereas Frost has spoken little about his favorite films or television series, Lynch's taste runs the gamut from studio-era Hollywood films, such as *Rear Window* (1954), *Sunset Boulevard* (1950), and *The Wizard of Oz* (1939) (Rodley 57, 71, 194), to the postwar European art cinemas of Federico Fellini, Ingmar Bergman, Werner Herzog, and Jacques Tati (62), to an auteur somewhere between those two worlds, Stanley Kubrick (77). Amazingly, Lynch does not consider himself a "film buff" (Murray 142).[11] With respect to *Twin Peaks*, one title does stand out among his moviegoing experiences: the Hollywood melodrama *A Summer Place* (1959), starring Sandra Dee and Troy Donohue. Lynch once told interviewers, when asked about the films of his youth, "It was fantastic to watch that kind of soap opera with your girlfriend. That made us dream!" (Ciment and Niogret 123).

Melodrama

We cannot know the degree to which *Peyton Place* and *A Summer Place* influenced *Twin Peaks*, but the comparisons are worth observing. Both films belong to the cycle of family melodramas that Hollywood produced in the 1950s and early 1960s, set in small towns or suburban environments, which intersected with two other melodrama cycles during the studio era: the 1950s juvenile delinquency film, such as Nicholas Ray's *Rebel without a Cause* (1955), and the "woman's film" or romantic "weepie," such as Sirk's *All That Heaven Allows* (1955), that began in the 1930s and 1940s. If the popularity of *Twin Peaks* paved the way for longer-running dramatic series about the goings-on of small towns, such as *Northern Exposure* (CBS, 1990–95), *Picket Fences* (CBS, 1992–96), *Desperate Housewives* (ABC, 2004–12), and *Pretty Little Liars* (Freeform, 2010–17), Hollywood's mid-century family melodramas opened the door for *Twin Peaks*. Not unlike how critics positioned the series "above" melodrama as an ironic, auteur-sanctioned soap opera, English-language film critics and academic film theorists of the 1970s and 1980s began taking Hollywood melodrama seriously through auteur-ist reappraisals of Sirk, Ray, and Vincente Minnelli. Rereading their family melodramas as critical of a capitalist society be-sieged by psychological, emotional, and sexual repression after World War II, film scholars found melodramatic excess capable of seeding a narrative cinema in opposition to dominant (i.e., bourgeois) norms of classical realism.

Melodrama encompasses a broader range of texts and aesthetic experiences, though, dating back to the eighteenth-century French and British stage when the monarchy adminis-tered patents to theaters to perform "legitimate," spoken-word plays. Without the aid of speech, unlicensed theaters had to rely entirely on music and physical performance to commu-nicate to the audience (the term "melodrama" derives from the Greek word for music, "melos," and the French word for drama, "drame"). Cinema continues this tradition of embod-ied spectator address and, according to Linda Williams, "reg-isters effects in the bodies of spectators" (4). "Woman's film" melodrama both displays "weeping" and "sobs of anguish," and also provokes "an almost involuntary mimicry of the emotion or sensation of the body on the screen" (4). Once deemed "un-official" theater for the middle- and working-class, the word "melodrama" has more recently been used as a pejorative term for "films addressed to women in their traditional status under patriarchy—as wives, mothers, abandoned lovers, or in their traditional status as bodily hysteria or excess, as in the frequent case of the woman 'afflicted' with a deadly or debilitating disease" (4). Williams attributes the "low cultural status" of melodrama to the woman's body as the primary on-screen embodiment of pain and sadness, and the source of the spectator's "overwhelming pathos" for suffering victimhood (4).

Chapter 4 will provide a close analysis of three melodramatic performances in *Twin Peaks*, but we must stress the pervasiveness of melodramatic bodies in the series. Younger cast members bring older stars to mind: Sherilyn Fenn's eighteen-year-old temptress Audrey bears a striking resemblance to Elizabeth Taylor, who at the age of seventeen starred in *A Place in the Sun* (1951), a film Lynch loves (Lynch and McKenna 238); James Marshall's teenage rebel, also named James, was inspired by *Rebel without a Cause* star James Dean (Hughes 110). By contrast, older stars return in self-referential roles: Russ Tamblyn, who plays Laura's psychiatrist Dr. Jacoby, earned an Academy Award nomination for Best Supporting Actor in *Peyton Place*; Jane Greer, who plays Norma's mean mother, had a recurring part on the prime-time soap opera *Falcon Crest* (CBS, 1981–90); and Ian Buchanan, who plays Lucy's ex-boyfriend Dick Tremayne, was a cast member on *General Hospital* (ABC, 1963-present).[12] We should add that Greer is best known as "femme fatale" Kathie Moffat from the noir classic *Out of the Past* (1947).

More significantly, the crying face became part of a melo-dramatic iconography in the series, both women's faces and (contrary to the masculinist conventions of prime-time television) the faces of men. Sheriff's Deputy Andy Brennan whimpers inconsolably when he discovers Laura's corpse washed ashore. Laura's father, Leland, clutches the sheriff and breaks down in

Donna Hayward (Lara Flynn Boyle) having a melodramatic moment (*Twin Peaks*, pilot).

tears when he learns of Laura's death, while her mother, Sarah, moans on the phone. Donna sobs in class when she realizes that Laura's empty chair means she may have lost her best friend. Even the high-school principal cannot help himself from openly weeping after he delivers the news over the PA system. And these examples are just from the pilot alone. The mournful, romantic keyboard music of "Laura Palmer's Theme" typically swells on the soundtrack to accompany such moments, underscoring emotional cues similar to the warbling of organs in early television soap operas.[13] Crying "cements identification," Lynch has said, as the experience "transfers over" from one person to another almost uncontrollably (Rodley 167).

Melodramatic pathos is tied not only to the spectacle of naked emotion on-screen but also to a particular narrative mode based on empathy and identification. Steve Neale claims that melodramas produce discrepancies in knowledge and point of view between spectator and characters (often the spectator knows more than the characters), and hinge on "chance happenings, coincidences, missed meetings, sudden conversions, last-minute rescues and revelations, *deus ex machina* endings" (6). Whatever the outcome, either happy ("just in time") or sad ("too late"), temporal delay puts the spectator in a position of powerlessness to change the order and motivation of narrative events (11–12). Tears ultimately express the spectator's feelings of fulfillment, loss, and the fantasy that fulfillment is still possible (21–22). The final melodramatic wish, "if only," simultaneously asks, "what if?" (22).

Episode 14 puts this convention to effect through crosscutting when Leland, under BOB's possession, murders Laura's twin cousin Maddy. Leland straightens his tie in the mirror and Lynch abruptly cuts to some of the principle characters (Donna, James, Bobby, Cooper, Truman, the Log Lady) listening to Julee Cruise sing in the Bang Bang Bar, nicknamed the "Roadhouse." The audience anxiously suspects the murder that is about to occur, but the characters remain unaware and therefore (like the audience) powerless to prevent it. When Cooper receives a warning from the Giant ("it is happening again"), Lynch cuts back to Leland/BOB, who restages Laura's murder by murdering Maddy, compounding the irreversible tragedy of the previous event for both the audience and Leland. Before administering the blow that finally kills her, he holds Maddy and cries "Laura." Back at the Roadhouse, the lyrics of Cruise's "The World Spins" achingly convey this "too late"/"if only" realization: "Love/Don't go away/Come back this way/Come back and stay/Forever and ever."

Donna's and Bobby's excessive reactions to Cruise's performance are entirely consistent with the melodramatic affect of this sequence. Ostensibly thinking about Harold Smith, the shut-in on her Meals on Wheels route who committed suicide earlier in the episode, Donna begins to cry, but Lara Flynn

Boyle's intensely overwrought performance suggests Donna has "felt" the double murder from her table at the Roadhouse along with the extradiegetic audience. Seated at the bar, Bobby meanwhile appears emotionally startled, but he did not know Harold and could not possibly know what happened to Maddy. Nevertheless, he, too, has somehow felt the loss the audience has experienced, a reaction made all the more poignant when one remembers his "if only"/"too late" diatribe during Laura's funeral: "You damn hypocrites make me sick! Everybody knew she was in trouble, but we didn't do anything. All you good people. You want to know who killed Laura? You did! We all did. And pretty words aren't going to bring her back, man, so save your prayers." As Robert Engels has said, *Twin Peaks* "was a TV show about free-floating guilt" (Rodley 156).

34

Reading *Twin Peaks* as earnest melodrama is not to deny an element of irony in the series, but this irony rarely serves the distancing effect *de rigueur* for critical appreciation. For example, characters in the first season watch a fictional daytime soap opera called *Invitation to Love*, which Frost wrote, directed, and shot on video in the historic Ennis House in Los Angeles. The self-consciously bad writing, acting, music, and costumes gently parody conventions of the soap opera, but never undermine the deployment of those very conventions in *Twin Peaks*. Rather, Frost's approach only throws this soap-within-a-soap into (comic) relief, calling attention to the embedded television screen as a *mise-en-abyme* and distinguishing *Invitation to Love* from *Twin Peaks* as a hypermediated and hyperbolic level of fiction within the diegesis.

Invitation to Love unites the people of Twin Peaks and mirrors the events of their lives, providing a cathartic way of negotiating the social conflicts of their everyday experiences and, paradoxically, an escape from those same conflicts. Perhaps, as the announcer opens each episode, one day will bring these characters "a new beginning" and hold "the promise of an invitation to love." Racked with grief over Laura's murder, Leland watches a father write a suicide note to his twin daughters (played by the same actress) when Maddy shows up to visit (Sheryl Lee played both Laura and Maddy). Shelly watches tough-guy Montana assault nerdy Chet, reflecting on her abusive husband Leo, who later sees Chet shoot Montana after he takes a bullet himself. Dr. Jacoby hears Montana toast to "old times," saying, "should old acquaintance be forgot," right before Maddy calls him, pretending to be his "old acquaintance" Laura. In Episode 4, when Sheriff Harry Truman asks Lucy "what's going on?" she excitedly briefs him on the most recent episode of *Invitation to Love* ("what's going on *here*?" he clarifies, referring to the "real" world of the Sheriff's Department). For these characters, *Invitation to Love* is as "real" as *Twin Peaks* is to its fans, even as fans see the mechanisms of melodrama exposed.

To encourage ABC to order a second season, Frost said he deliberately incorporated every conceivable cliffhanger from "the history of the nighttime soap" in Episode 7, the finale of the first season, which he both wrote and directed ("Secrets"). Frost intended to reach a level of absurdity with the sheer accretion of genre conventions, but at the same time he sought to achieve "as much edge-of-the-seat tension" as possible ("Secrets"). As Lucy recaps in Episode 8, this time summarizing the events of *Twin Peaks*, "Leo Johnson was shot, Jacques Renault was strangled, the mill burned, Shelly and Pete got smoke inhalation, Catherine and Josie are missing, Nadine is in a coma from taking sleeping pills." Lucy also discovers she is pregnant and uncertain of the father's identity. The finale of the first season ultimately (if only temporarily) shifted the central question of the series from "Who killed Laura Palmer?" to "Who shot Agent Cooper?" Protected by his bullet-proof vest, Cooper is rescued "just in time" when Harry, Andy, and Hawk find him bleeding and barely conscious on the floor of his hotel room at the beginning of Episode 8.

Noir

Cooper, the straight-arrow, big-city investigator assigned to the Laura Palmer case, links *Twin Peaks* with two approximate cycles of Hollywood film noir in the 1940s: the private-eye or "lone wolf" phase during World War II and the more realistic police procedurals of the postwar period (Schrader 58–59). Entering Twin Peaks in the pilot, a town that seems frozen in the 1940s or 1950s, he "retreats to the past" (58), and with his tape-recorded messages to his secretary Diane, he bespeaks "a love of romantic narration" (57). After manipulating time in Parts 17 and 18, he triggers "a complex chronological order" in *Twin Peaks* that "reinforce[s] the feelings of hopelessness and lost time," leaving characters temporally disoriented and literally in the dark (58).

Frost, Lynch, and the various directors of the series occasionally lend a stylized noir "look," as well. The exterior shots of Snoqualmie Falls give the series an "an almost Freudian attachment to water," surging under the Great Northern Hotel and into the river that carried Laura's body, reminiscent of the docks, piers, and rain-swept streets of classic noir. Low-key, high-contrast lighting and interior scenes lit for night establish a fatalistic atmosphere, with actors "standing in the shadow," such as when characters pass through the convenience store to visit Phillip Jeffries or emerge from blackness in the subterranean basement of the Great Northern. Lighting cuts through windows in oblique lines and "odd shapes" to "splinter a screen," such as the chiaroscuro effect inside the Horne's Department Store closet, where Audrey hides to spy on the manager in Episode 6. Canted camera angles create an oblique frame and make the screen appear "restless and unstable," such as when Josie answers a threatening phone call from Hank at the end of Episode 4 (Schrader 57). Encoded in *Twin Peaks* are well-known noir intertexts that critics have enjoyed spotting, including namesakes from *Double Indemnity* (1944) and *Laura*

Low-key, high-contrast lighting on Sherilyn Fenn as Audrey Horne (*Twin Peaks*, Episode 6).

(1944). Twin Peaks is also the name of a real site in San Francisco and the primary setting of *Experiment in Terror* (1962), an FBI procedural about a killer—named Garland Lynch—stalking a young female bank teller, whom he wants to coerce into stealing $100,000 for him. In case one forgets that Gordon Cole was a minor character in *Sunset Boulevard* who worked in the Paramount Pictures prop department, Cooper/Dougie catches the film on television in Part 15. (Recognizing the name "Gordon Cole," Dougie electrocutes himself and awakens Cooper.)

The aforementioned narrative and stylistic conventions, as articulated by Paul Schrader writing in 1972, have become part of the conventional wisdom about film noir. However, revisionist scholarly interventions have contextualized noir in a less linear or coherent history, pointing out that its body of films is more narratively and thematically diverse and their expressionistic visual style is not as uniform as previously assumed (see Nare-more, *More than Night*). Vivian Sobchack argues that aesthetic histories have not sufficiently accounted for the phenomenol-ogy of particular, materially grounded places in the US after World War II that comprise the *mise-en-scène* of noir set in both urban and small-town locations: boardinghouses and cheap roadside motels, diners and dive bars, nightclubs and cock-tail lounges, gas and transit stations, and the lonely roads in between. At a time when President Truman's administration promoted postwar stability and a consolidation of interna-tional power, domestic anxieties simmered over the shortage of housing and the increase of rent, the rising costs of food and clothing, the spread of communism, and the possibilities of a renewed Depression (Sobchack 132). Note that Harry S. Tru-man, the baby boomer–era sheriff who presides over law and order in Twin Peaks, shares the same name as the first president of the United States after World War II.

The universe of *Twin Peaks* exists in the noir-esque shadow of the atomic bomb, the origin of modern trauma, according to Part 8's black-and-white "creation story" that begins, paradoxi-cally, with the apocalyptic image of the 1945 "Trinity" nuclear test in White Sands, New Mexico. Characters desire to go home and continually seek a "mythological construction," "the idyllic wartime home front" that "stands as this country's lost object of desire" (Sobchack 133). Quoting from *The Wizard of Oz*, Sob-chack's double entendre, "'there is no place like home'" (137), highlights the "dislocation, isolation, and existential alienation" of these "no places" that characters inhabit (155). It is not inci-dental that when evil hatches in New Mexico eleven years after "Trinity" (in the form of a froglike insect), it invades young Sarah Palmer's house, and that at the beginning of *The Return*, the Fireman/Giant tells Cooper, "It is in our house now."

In *Twin Peaks*, nocturnal postwar trauma sends shock waves that ripple up to the present in the light of day—"the past dic-tates the future," as Cooper explains—and the inky places that mark the geography of this history turn leisure into "idle restlessness" (Sobchack 158). Diners such as Hap's and Eat at Judy's are inhospitable at best, and Pop's Diner in New Mexico is immediately affected by the Woodsman's anesthetizing broadcast. Gas stations are earth-based versions of the red-curtained "waiting room"; at Big Ed's Gas Farm, Ed nurses a cup of soup in the back office, pining after Norma late into the night. Bored young people wile away their time listening to nightly bands at the Roadhouse, where fights break out, bartenders enable prostitution, and corrupt cops pocket bribe money. A chance encounter at a rustic tavern called Wallies lures James into a mariticide plot à la *Double Indemnity*. Diane regularly drinks alone at Max Von's Bar, while Sarah tears into the jugular of a sexist trucker at the Elk's Point #9 Bar who won't leave her alone. Brothel and casino One Eyed Jack's facilitates drug smuggling and kidnapping, to say nothing of the exploitation of the women it employs.

Motels are places of sordid rendezvous, savage violence, and unexplained happenings. Ben and Catherine carry on their affair at the Timber Falls Motel, where they conspire to burn down the Packard Saw Mill. Leland makes secret appointments with prostitute Teresa Banks at the Red Diamond City Motel, and Mr. C brutally kills his criminal partner Darya at an unnamed motel in South Dakota. Phillip Jeffries hides in an old gangster hangout that no longer occupies physical space, a motel called The Dutchman's Lodge, accessible through the darkest postwar "no place" of *Twin Peaks*, a convenience store next to an abandoned gas station guarded by Woodsmen. Spirits are said to hold meetings in a room above the store. Most unsettling of all is the midcentury motel where Cooper and Diane stay in Part 18. After a night of passionless sex, Cooper awakens in a different motel with Diane gone, and finds a letter from "Linda" (formerly Diane) that refers to him as "Richard." Indeed, as Albert informs Tammy, the first Blue Rose Case involved an occurrence involving doubles in a motel.

Places of residence do not offer the safety, stability, and nurturing environment of a home. Dead Dog Farm houses only drug deals. Harold Smith's house is more of a prison, next door to the suspicious Mrs. Tremond and her grandson, who may be spirits named Chalfont. The psychotic Richard Horne disrupts domestic space, viciously attacking a witness to a hit-and-run and, later, his own grandmother, in Part 10. Whereas Donna's idyllic house is violated (first by BOB in Episode 9, then by Windom Earle in Episode 24), Shelly lives with an abusive husband in a house under permanent renovation. Grim ironies seep from the Fat Trout Trailer Park; one resident complains that the government has barely been able to provide his wife (a disabled veteran) with an adequate wheelchair, while another sells his blood in order to afford food. The warm, comforting Double R Diner is the closest place Twin Peaks has to a home, but as a roadside diner, it is only a transient place, a stop-off point on the way somewhere else, and its nourishments are therefore temporary. Down in Odessa, Texas, Carrie Page cannot wait to leave home—a man's dead body sits on her couch, never commented upon, with a bullet hole in the middle of his head.

Frost has explained that he wanted the 2008–9 economic recession to frame Cooper's Odyssean journey in *The Return* (all the way to Odessa), requiring a more expansive national landscape beyond the town of Twin Peaks. The Rancho Rosa Estates in Las Vegas are a fictional example of the "vast tracked housing developments that had been built in the anticipation of this endless boom and were then abandoned" (O'Falt). If the series is a belated postwar noir, these "three-year-old-ghost towns" also give *The Return* purchase in cultural crisis of the early twenty-first century (O'Falt). Not without affection for their characters or belief in human potential, Frost and Lynch draw hopeful closure around the Jones family story line at the beginning of Part 18, albeit away from Twin Peaks in suburban Las Vegas. This touching resolution is short-lived and somewhat misleading, coming at the beginning of Part 18 rather than the end, with Cooper's tulpa back at the elusive "red door" in Lancelot Court to stay permanently with Janey-E and her son, Sonny Jim.

All the narrative roads lead to the Palmers' 1930s Dutch colonial revival house, but the return at the end of Part 18 is not the homecoming audiences saw in the Jones household, belying Cooper's confident assurance to Laura at the end of Part 17, "we're going home." Frost's *Twin Peaks: The Final Dossier* (2017) states that Cooper's one character flaw is his "irresistible urge to rescue every damsel in distress he came across," and the Arthurian place names hint at this "white knight syndrome" (57). Prior to the events of Season 1, Cooper failed to protect a woman named Caroline, a material witness in a federal crime, and he blamed himself for his lack of preparation because he fell in love with her. Season 2 ends with him unable to save the new woman he loves, Annie, from his deranged former partner, Windom Earle, Caroline's murderer and husband. The hubris Cooper displays in tempting fate (O'Falt), hoping to save Laura, rewrite her story, and bring her home to her mother, does not grant him absolution of his mistakes but instead dredges them up from out of the past. The new owner of the house, Alice Tremond, does not know Sarah or recognize Laura and confirms that no one by the name "Palmer" has owned the house in recent years.[14] Noir fatalism collides with the melodramatic "if only" in the last spoken line of the series. "What year is this?" Cooper asks. Faced with the site of her own trauma, Laura must relive the experience of her murder through her new identity as Carrie Page. Laura may be dead, but she lives, *here* but *not* here, and in "no place."

41

"I am dead, yet I live"

Femmes Fatales and the Women of Twin Peaks

Laura Palmer as femme fatale is the central figure of the *Twin Peaks* cycle—its traumatized muse—throughout its initial seasons and "return." Mark Frost and David Lynch's continual rewriting of her fate helps to clarify the figure of the femme fatale, which is also always shifting, as representations of women mediate the intersections between female and dominant cultures. Constantly brought back to life, the femme fatale, like Laura Palmer in her "returns" within the *Twin Peaks* universe, destabilizes the fixed identities of narrative and character patterns, as well as sources and their continuations. *Twin Peaks* provides some key understanding of the ideation surrounding the femme fatale, whose relentless *presence* as a threat to conventional images of femininity and masculinity depends in some sense on *absence*, on a myth characterized by the opacity, aloofness, and mysteriousness that constitute ambiguity and paradox.

In the first episode of *The Return*, Sheryl Lee, reprising her role as Laura Palmer more than twenty-five years after the character was purportedly killed by her father, Leland, possessed by the demon BOB, sits beside Agent Cooper in the Red Room.

In this oneiric setting, Laura tells Cooper that she is here, and not here: "I am dead, yet I live." Laura's contradictory ontology links with her namesake Laura Hunt (Gene Tierney), who was also provocatively there in the story of *Laura* (1944) and not there. The ambiguities surrounding women's identities, and the show's insistence on breaking down categories of female presence, constitute a critique of the objectification of women and the men who seek confirmation of their own power in their gender fantasies.

One of the most iconic of femmes fatales in original-cycle film noir, Laura Hunt provides an important intertext for Laura Palmer. Like her homecoming queen picture, framed to project her would-be normalcy and innocence, the image of Laura Palmer is the major figure presiding over the world of Twin Peaks, just as Tierney's Laura dominates the *mise-en-scène* in *Laura,* seducing Detective Mark McPherson (Dana Andrews) as an image before Tierney appears in the film's present time to puncture the illusion of perfect female "to-be-looked-at-ness," to borrow Laura Mulvey's well-known phrase (11). *Twin Peaks* adapts the woman-as-picture motif to explore the potential for a macabre objectification of women, whose performances as sexual provocateurs are a means of survival as well as a form of rebellion against being controlled by men.

Beyond the major role of Laura Palmer, *Twin Peaks* extends its critique of cultural obsessions with "good" and "bad" women in a number of female characters that invoke the figure of the femme fatale. For example, following Laura's death, her "good-girl" best friend Donna Hayward assumes the role of the femme fatale in Episode 8. Donna tries on the role of seducer as a means of identifying melodramatically with Laura. In love with Laura's secret boyfriend, James Hurley, Donna wonders about the "other side," wishing to explore an alternative identity to her own girl-next-door persona. When Donna visits James in jail wearing Laura's dark sunglasses, she tells him she has started smoking because it "helps relieve tension." James's

43

resistance to Donna's seduction brings to the surface a dynamic repeatedly explored by *Twin Peaks*: women try to break out of roles that feel claustrophobic or oppressive and are rejected or harmed when they seek to shift their identities or express their desires. Donna challenges James on this point, when she senses his withdrawal, asking him, "What's wrong? [. . .] Or is it just not okay for me to want you?" Lara Flynn Boyle's comments in 1990 underscore the layered quality of her character: "Donna was a little sad, dull, lifeless, boring, and comatose. [. . .] But there's a lot of fire underneath" (Zehme 72).

There are two motivations for the focus in *Twin Peaks* on the femme fatale figure: one, to emphasize women's desire for liberation, a release from their prescribed roles and unfulfilling lives; and two, to critique the dynamic in which men project ideation onto women in order to ensure or reinforce patriarchal control. Both of these themes are familiar motifs in classic film noir (see Grossman, *Rethinking*), and both are central ways through which *Twin Peaks* exposes gender trauma and the harrowing attempts of women to control their own destinies. In the penultimate episode of *The Return*, the show flashes back to a scene in *Twin Peaks: Fire Walk with Me* just before Laura's death when she tells James, "Your Laura disappeared. It's just me now." Laura's tortured revelation to James echoes film noir's continual presentation of "fatal women" as individuals scheming to evade male attempts to categorize, objectify, and oppress or victimize them. As Laura suggests to James, women transgress often to insist on being seen for who they are, not the fantasies their lovers want them to be. The series seems to endorse Laura's critique of such solipsistic projection, echoing femme fatale Kathie Moffat (Jane Greer) in *Out of the Past*, who reminds Jeff Markham after he discovers her betrayal, "I never told you anything but what I am. You just wanted to imagine I was. That's why I left you." It is worth noting that Catherine Martell explains the character of another femme-fatale figure, Josie Packard, in similar terms of women navigating what and who men want them to be. From early on, Josie had to "survive by being what other people wanted to see." While her guileless lover, Sheriff Harry Truman, responded to Josie simply, "She was so beautiful," Catherine suggests a more complicated negotiation and conciliation: "what she needed to believe was always shifting to suit the moment" (Episode 26).

The presence of the femme fatale in *Twin Peaks* thus has meaning beyond providing mere titillation. As in classic film noir, the women of *Twin Peaks* perform roles to rebel against being oppressed, either to gain empowerment otherwise denied them or as a means of survival. Femmes fatales perform different identities, as do Donna and Maddy, Laura's look-alike cousin: they take on new or varied roles to evade preconceived notions about them or they "put on a show" to give their "audience" what they want (as Gilda does in her performance of "Put the Blame on Mame" in *Gilda* [1946]). Laura admits to her own repeated performance as seducer in the "What's Up Doc?" tape in Episode 6: "Why is it so easy to make men like me?"

Laura's appearance throughout *Twin Peaks* vacillates among the various incarnations of the femme fatale: in the Red Room in *The Return*, Laura whispers seductively in Cooper's ear and kisses him, but her final shriek is a shocking "return" for viewers to the Laura of *Twin Peaks: Fire Walk with Me*, in which we experience quite viscerally a young woman utterly traumatized by men, fathers, sexual predators, and demons. *Twin Peaks: Fire Walk with Me* uncannily deconstructs the victimization of women commonly labeled as "femmes fatales." Laura's imprint as a character depends on her interrogation of the classic femme fatale role: coded throughout the *Twin Peaks* universe as a figure of female innocence and desire, she is a complex victim of violent and psychopathic exploitation, incest, and assault.

Complementing this representation, in *Twin Peaks: Fire Walk with Me*, Leland Palmer is a more extreme version of the men in classic and neo-noir (Johnny Farrell, Mark McPherson, Jake Gittes, Travis Bickle) who project their own mistrust of women onto them, causing them distress or harm. These men are tormented by their ideation, attracted to, repelled, and compelled by women with charisma, whose sexuality they see only as a danger to themselves.

Trapped, as many women of *Twin Peaks* are, within a pattern of wanting something more than what life affords them, Laura's dark-haired cousin Madeleine "Maddy" Ferguson (also Lee) recognizes in one moment the frisson of "playing" Laura, when James and Donna have Maddy pose as Laura to entice and discover the killer (Episode 6). In Episode 9, as James sings "Just You and I" with Maddy and Donna harmonizing, Donna observes and is upset by Maddy's seductive sidelong glance at James. In this moment, the wallflower Maddy emulates Laura's sexual provocation. As she later tells James, "For a while I got to be somebody different." Maddy, whose name is a reference to another female absent presence, Madeleine Elster in *Vertigo* (1958), appears in a line of spirited and endangered women.

Like the doomed women in *Vertigo*, Laura and Maddy are inextricably linked to their charisma and their danger, as much *from* men as to them. As Judy is implored by Scottie Ferguson (James Stewart) that "it can't matter" to her if he molds and manipulates her human form into an image of another woman he loved and mourns, Maddy knows she must escape Twin Peaks to maintain her selfhood; when she tells Leland and Sarah Palmer she's leaving, she says it's because "I miss having a life of my own." Maddy doesn't manage to escape before Leland/ BOB acts on his obsession with punishing vibrant women, killing Maddy in one of the most sorrowful scenes in the series (Episode 14).

In these visual and aural evocations of film noir's classic femmes fatales, *Twin Peaks* imagines a bond among them, women who understand one another's trials and traumas. This insight helps us to process some of *The Return*'s uncanny moments, such as one scene in which Shelly Briggs (formerly Johnson) and Norma Jennings stand together in the diner, watching

Shelly Briggs (Mädchen Amick) and Norma Jennings (Peggy Lipton) in solidarity (*The Return*, Part 5).

Becky be manipulated by her dissolute husband, Steven. The curtains on the window frame this picture of active female observation and solidarity.

In no character is the femme fatale more poignantly invoked than in the role of Audrey Horne, whom *Entertainment Weekly's* Ken Tucker dubbed a "sloe-eyed bad girl" (8) when *Twin Peaks* first premiered. In Seasons 1 and 2, Audrey is presented as seductive and provocative, but also clever and intuitive, matching Cooper's own detective skills. In Episode 5, we see Audrey's dynamism, complexity, and depth. In the middle of the episode, she watches her father plotting with Catherine from a secret hiding place; she spies on the two through a peephole. Intrigued by illicit adult behavior, Audrey is excited to see Catherine slap Ben, as the light shines on the teen voyeur's eyes. But it is Audrey's variability that makes her a strong and powerful character: she sees the irony and humor in absurd settings, but has a genuine infatuation with Cooper because she recognizes his difference from everything around her, and he responds to her vulnerability, seeing in her something beyond a teen vamp. Audrey has financial resources, unlike many of the down-and-out women in film noir, but she inhabits the psychology of the femme fatale role in other ways, in her "toxic beauty" (Zehme 72), often accompanied by distress and a satiric tone or dismissive attitude toward men. In Episode 20, we see Audrey's toughness and her resistance to male control. "Don't worry baby. Bobby's on the case," Bobby says to Audrey about Ben's mental illness, after Bobby joins the managerial team at the Great Northern. Audrey deflates Bobby's bid to use the sexist verbal patterns we remember from classic film noir ("I'm crazy about you, baby," smarms Walter Neff in *Double Indemnity* [see Evans]). "Don't call me 'baby,'" Audrey says to Bobby, as they walk offscreen. Audrey must contend with not only her father's control and corrupt manipulation but Bobby's obliviousness to her ambition as a working professional. It is also worth noting that the last we see of Audrey in Season 2 is her engaging in civil disobedience, locking herself to a safe at the bank in a strong activist gesture of rebellion against capitalist exploitations.

Like the female characters played with toughness and vulnerability in film noir, Audrey is looking for meaning, excitement, and an outlet for her intellect, talent, and desire. In classic film noir, *Gun Crazy*'s Annie Laurie Starr (1950; Peggy Cummins) commands viewers' attention because, like Vera in *Detour* (1945), she yells her demands and her desires. In *Gun Crazy*, Annie Laurie shouts, "I want action!" But often, femmes fatales also register the damaging emotional consequences of wanting to escape prescribed and rigid social roles, or the inflexible judgment of others. While Al Roberts calls Vera "rotten" in *Detour*, she's got tuberculosis. Her acerbic tone is linked to wanting more from life before she's dead: "Life's like a ball game. You gotta take a swing at whatever comes along before you find it's the ninth inning." Vera's compellingly caustic delivery is a thin cover for the trauma at the margins of the American Dream she represents.

Audrey understands the trauma held within Twin Peaks. In Episode 6, Ben tries to disguise Leland's breakdown following Laura's murder from his Icelandic business colleagues visiting the Great Northern. While Audrey watches the tortured Leland grab his head and emotionally dissolve, dancing and crying outrageously at the party, Catherine covers for Leland (and Ben), pretending that his wail is part of a dance. Holding her own head beside him, she joins the dance in a macabre exploitation of his suffering. Audrey cries as she observes this excessive display of anguish and performance.

In the next episode, she continues her detective work, proving her credentials as a sexualized woman at One Eyed Jack's when she ties the stem of a cherry into a knot with her tongue. This seductively erotic dimension of Audrey's character is reinforced by what Ben tells Cooper: "Men fall under the spell of Audrey's charms like ducks in a shooting gallery" (Episode 10). Audrey's sheer determination ("I'm Audrey Horne and I get what I want," she says to the sexist manager of Horne's Department Store) defines her role as an active, provocative, and potentially dangerous character.

As with Laura, however, Audrey's role-playing hardly disguises her yearning and innocence, which may explain her identification with Laura. "I understood her," Audrey says about Laura in Episode 3, an identification that takes on added dimension after the threat of incest emerges when Ben pursues a masked Audrey at One Eyed Jack's. In Episode 8, underscoring her vulnerability and desire for connection, Audrey says about Ben: "All I ever really wanted was for him to love me."

In *The Return*, we don't see Audrey until Part 12, at which point she is trapped, possibly within a dream or a mental asylum. "Doc" Haywood had earlier told Frank Truman in Part 7 that Audrey was in a coma after the explosion in the bank ended Season 2. Cooper, who was "acting mighty strange," went to visit her, an ominous suggestion that Audrey was raped by Mr. C, leading presumably to the birth of a depraved son,

Richard. The painful conversations between Audrey and her husband, Charlie, focused as they are on Audrey's frustration, anger, and thwarted desires, challenge viewers because Lynch prolongs the uncomfortable exchanges for so long, trapping us within these scenes to mirror Audrey's own imprisonment and desperation. In the second of these exchanges, Audrey hints more particularly at a condition that could be a mental disorder: "I feel like I'm somewhere else [. . .] and like I'm somebody else"; "I'm not sure who I am but I'm not me"; "Who am I supposed to trust but myself and I don't even know who I am." Charlie responds to Audrey's doubt about her identity with the strange threat, "now, are you going to stop playing games or do I have to end your story too?" Audrey's paralysis—she is unable to stay in the house but seems also incapable of leaving—is

linked to the idea that her despair derives from someone else controlling the narrative of her life. This makes particular sense regarding Audrey, since her girl-detective persona has always reflected her attempt to discover things on her own and, in the original series, as Martha Nochimson rightly observes, "part of her legitimate desire to participate in a world from which her father's ruthless domination of the town threatens to exclude her" (150). Instead, here, late in *The Return*, she is immobilized and told that her husband will rewrite her story. Her devastation is intimately tied to her being trapped within roles defined by others, a repeated theme for women throughout *Twin Peaks*.

Audrey's appearance in *The Return* culminates in her dance at the Roadhouse. Introduced by the MC, "Ladies and Gentlemen, 'Audrey's Dance,'" she takes the floor as everyone clears away and her theme music begins. Others at the Roadhouse sway dreamily as Audrey dances, intoxicated by her sensual and powerful reprise of the voluptuous dance whose excess we marveled at in Episode 2. When her entranced dancing at the Roadhouse is abruptly interrupted by a brawl ensuing at the bar, Audrey rushes to Charlie and says in a panic, "Get me out of here!" Lynch cuts from a close-up of a distraught Audrey to a reflection of her face in a mirror surrounded by the white garb and walls associated with asylums. A despairing Audrey, facing the image of herself scrubbed of makeup, says, "What? What? What?" On the one hand, viewers are brought into the *mise-en-abyme* of Audrey's desolation, and this sequence is certainly in keeping with the show's insistence on shifting the ontological ground on which these characters tread. The final scene with Audrey follows up on her earlier questioning of her identity, suggesting a dissolution of Audrey's self, or madness. On the other hand, this finale reminds one of Norma Desmond's last gestures in *Sunset Boulevard*. Both femmes fatales stage a final victory in performing an illusion. Madness seems the tragic recourse for women pummeled by life, but the two stories allow for female imagination and expression within that traumatized state to enable moments of liberation: Norma's fantasy as an aging film star that she is back in the game and Audrey's pure pleasure in having her body and her environment be in total sync as she takes command of the scene at the Roadhouse. The rhythm and moves of *Twin Peaks*'s vibrant female seeker establish deep empathy for Audrey and appreciation for her charisma and heart.

The central concern of *Twin Peaks* with strong yet damaged women helps us to understand other memorable scenes. Like Audrey, Sheriff Frank Truman's wife, Doris, harangues her husband about his failure to help her and give her what she wants. The brutish officer Chad verbally pounces on her, implying that she is a shrew, and Maggie, the switchboard operator, upbraids him, saying, "She didn't used to be like this." Doris has never been the same since the Trumans' son committed suicide. This resonates with Leland's comments when he is arrested in Episode 11 and he describes the "absolute loss" of witnessing the death of a child: "Every cell screams. You can hear nothing else."

Like Doris, yet a more central character, Janey-E Jones may at first blush appear to be a nagging wife; however, she comes to embody the vibrant female energy so predominant in *Twin*

Sherilyn Fenn as Audrey Horne, reprising her celebrated trance-dance (*The Return*, Part 16).

Peaks. The complaints of Janey-E fill the void in the scenes in which she and Dougie appear. She occupies the vacuous space created by Cooper's fractured self, his withdrawn affect as Dougie soliciting her active response. If old Dougie was self-involved, his profligacy causing Janie-E to suffer, Cooper's version of Dougie opens up the possibility for her to have agency and to achieve her desires, surely exemplified in the sex scene in Part 10 in which her screaming with pleasure recasts the anguished screams of Laura Palmer.

Moreover, it is the lovable, intrepid Janey-E who pays Dougie's gambling debts, meeting with two thugs in a park in an effort to protect the Jones family. She has had to contend not only with Dougie's adultery but with a gambling habit that has threatened the safety and well-being of the family. Instrumental in pushing the story forward, Janey-E lambastes the criminals for exploiting the Joneses, telling them exactly how much interest she is willing to pay on the principal loan (less than was demanded), angrily telling the flummoxed criminals that she and Dougie are the depleted troops of the "ninety-ninth percentile." "We drive terrible cars!" she insists. The scene exemplifies Frost's stated intention to contextualize *The Return* in a post-2008 US riven by income inequality and economic stress (see O'Falt). Viewers may be enticed by cultural stereotypes to misread strong yet traumatized women characters, but they might also miss these important moments of empathy, a crucial element in *Twin Peaks*'s representation of not only the suffering of women but also female frustration and resilience.

One major instance of this dynamic regards once again *Sunset Boulevard* and its iconic female protagonist, whose visit with "Mr. DeMille" at Paramount is seen on television in the background in Part 16. Frost and Lynch's subtitle—it's *Twin Peaks: The Return*—is another homage to Billy Wilder's 1950 film. We remember that Norma Desmond insists that her resumption of acting be called a "return" and not a "comeback" ("I hate that word!" she says). Norma wants a reboot. The return of Laura Palmer similarly grapples with contradictory emotions of presence and loss, the paradox of celluloid and televisual eternality, and the performer's confrontation with mortality and aging, like Norma's melodramatic rising up into the projector's light after showing Joe Gillis the film *Queen Kelly* (in which Swanson herself starred in 1929), directed by Erich von Stroheim (who plays Norma's butler, Max Von Mayerling).

In its further preoccupation with Norma Desmond, *The Return* calls to mind the trials faced by female performers, for whom the pressure to be enchanting in Hollywood before they "age out" is as much a reality now as it was in the studio era. Dennis Lim recounts how ABC objected in 1998 to Lynch's casting of Naomi Watts (then thirty) and Laura Harring (then thirty-four) in negotiations surrounding the initial plan to broadcast *Mulholland Drive* on television; they were seen by studio executives as "too old" (147). Frost and Lynch resist industry norms and pay tribute instead to powerful older femmes, Peggy Lipton's Norma, Sherilyn Fenn's Audrey, Mädchen Amick's Shelly, and Watts's Janey-E. In addition to age norms, *Twin Peaks* also problematizes the binary between male and female that Hollywood insists upon. David Duchovny of *The X-Files* fame plays transgender DEA agent Denise Bryson, who rises through the ranks to FBI chief of staff twenty-five years later.

More existentially, *Twin Peaks* features Norma Desmond to ally her with Laura Palmer and other women in the series who share the acute pain of being neither fully alive nor fully dead, returning us to this chapter's title. Norma and Laura reside in liminal spaces, their past selves haunting an always vulnerable present in living-room pictures. Just after Laura says to Cooper, "I am dead, yet I live," she kisses him—the picture of Laura(s) coming alive to the senses. She whispers to him, then she begins to shake violently, releases her signature scream, and is whisked away into the atmosphere. Never able to maintain control, Laura, like Norma Desmond and many of film noir's other femmes fatales, nevertheless tries continually to grasp and express some mastery of her experience, when alive, or dead, or even living in Odessa, Texas, as the mysterious Carrie Page.

Norma Jennings seems far from a femme fatale figure, but her name is reminiscent of Norma Desmond, and the two similarly animate the idea of female longing. Like Norma Desmond, Norma Jennings lives in the past, mourning the loss of her lover Ed Hurley. But Norma is primarily identified through her business and the pride she takes in her coffee and pie. As an entrepreneur threatened by commercial franchise in *The Return*, Norma also brings to mind Cora Smith (Lana Turner) from *The Postman Always Rings Twice* (1946)—oppressed by a brutish husband in the first two seasons, Norma strives for significance through her business, as Cora seeks to do. Note that Cora's diner is called the "Twin Oaks." Echoing famous femmes fatales from film noir, Norma Jennings emphasizes their humanity: the noir women's creativity and efforts to find meaning and success through their labor.

If Norma, Audrey, Laura Palmer, Donna, and Maddy distill certain elements of the femme fatale, Laura Dern's Diane adds significantly to the show's portrait of dangerous and doomed women to underscore and show empathy for female trauma. In the first two seasons, Diane doesn't have a voice or a face. Associated in *The Return* with another woman without a face (Naido, whose name is a sort of anagram of "Diane"), here Diane breaks out and breaks bad. She represents another version of the femme fatale figure: the hard-boiled woman who takes no guff ("Fuck you, Albert"), enjoys a "stable of male suitors" (Part 10), and breaks rules (smoking indoors and on airplanes). Introduced by Gordon Cole as a "tough cookie" (Part 7), Diane is also broken, and insolence masks her trauma.

There is, after all, a reason why Lynch and Frost have long identified with the story of Marilyn Monroe, having begun their collaboration with an unproduced adaptation of Anthony Summers's *Goddess: The Secret Lives of Marilyn Monroe*. Lynch, in particular, cathects on Monroe, her vulnerability and tragedy, revealing in *Room to Dream*, "You could say that Laura Palmer is Marilyn Monroe, and that *Mulholland Drive* is about Marilyn Monroe, too. Everything is about Marilyn Monroe" (272). A magnet for exploitative ideation (the performer herself having said, "I was always bumping into people's unconscious" [MacCannell 124]), Monroe captures for Lynch a dynamic whereby vulnerable and charismatic women are trapped by systemic objectification and victimization. So, too, the Diane who was a devoted partner to Cooper in Seasons 1 and 2 and *Twin Peaks: Fire Walk with Me* has been wounded and betrayed by predatory men. In *The Return*, Diane, raped in a previous time by Mr. C, presents another version of the stories of Monroes and Lauras and Madeleines: copies, tulpas, of women exploited by a system where patriarchy, sexual predation, capitalism, and American hubris collude in damaging women, who are then filled with rage and sorrow. Diane's revelation to the Blue Rose team concerning the night Cooper raped her is painful and emotional. The powerful effect of Diane's admission is due in part to Dern's gripping performance, including, in an echo of

55

Audrey's complaint to Charlie about her lost self, Diane's agonized cry, "I'm not me. I'm not me!" The scene also reveals Diane's betrayal by a person she idolized, Agent Cooper. Such disappointment has caused Diane's cynicism, a pattern long associated with film noir characters. But this disillusionment is tied directly to gender and trauma here, establishing Diane, as well as Audrey and Laura, as powerfully duped by the insufficient fairy tales that have guided their "normal" psychosocial lives.

Sarah Palmer, too, enacts female rage, reinforcing a major component of the classic femme fatale: she is paradoxically the victim and the source of violence. The witch-like Sarah smokes Salem cigarettes and seems possessed by the evil force Judy. But the suppressed rage she shows in later episodes of *The Return* accompanies a devastation and loneliness also clear in Grace Zabriskie's magnetic performance. Sarah's agitation in the grocery store scene, and her disgust and clenched mouth voicing a barely suppressed fury at Hawk's inquiry when he shows up at her door, is spellbinding to watch. Seething with rage and irony, Sarah dismisses the normalcy represented by Hawk's visit and concern: "I just don't know what came over me"; "It's a goddamn bad story, isn't it Hawk." Lindsay Hallam observes that Zabriskie's awareness of Sarah's "lonely existence" speaks to "a sad indictment of society's marginalization and disinterest in women as they age, but also stands as a testament to how Sarah has been forgotten when dealing with the events that tore her family apart" (*Twin Peaks* 111). When a vulgar misogynist whose T-shirt reads "Truck You" sits at the bar beside her in Part 14 of *The Return*, this fatal woman punishes him for his vile words and attitude by opening up her face to reveal the wrath within her. And then she rips his neck off. As the bartender expresses suspicion about her role in the gruesome incident, Sarah is again dismissive and ironic: "Sure is a mystery." *The Return* thus contextualizes Sarah's ferocity (she watches circular loops on TV of boxing and tigers eating one another) in a scene of toxic misogyny and reinforces the idea that Sarah's violence cannot be divorced from the trauma and violence that have defined her.

Throughout *Twin Peaks*, individuals are vulnerable to being erased or replicated by those with greater power or authority. MIKE tells Dougie in Part 3 of *The Return* that "someone manufactured you." When he says these words to Diane in Part 16, however, the comment carries additional force, resonating further with the series' exposure of men processing women as images they can control. These women are then punished for exceeding the boundaries of male ideation with desires of their own. To use the language of Hitchcock's *Shadow of a Doubt* (1943), *Twin Peaks* "[rips] the fronts off houses" to reveal the monstrous nature of casting women as suburban or sexual idols, part of the push to mythologize within the US. In this repetition-compulsion-based need to make present women absent, first by mythifying them as femmes fatales, and then killing them off, or sending them to the insane asylum (Norma Desmond, Audrey Horne), Laura's repeated shriek—decades of wailing, culminating in the final scream at the series' end—seems an apt manifestation of revolt.

The presence of versions of the femme fatale is crucial to the worlds of *Twin Peaks*, mainly because these figures distill the fundamental poles of affect and experience in Frost and Lynch's universe: liberation and trauma. These female characters and their tulpas, their voices, and their dynamic movement—Laura's reappearances and resilience; Audrey's dance and Nancy Drew–detective verve; Diane's hard-boiled toughness and recalcitrance—constitute a resistance to objectification and victimization, leaving us with the powerful energy of the women at the heart of *Twin Peaks*.

4

Acting Strangely

Three Performances in Twin Peaks

The deconstructed figure of the femme fatale in *Twin Peaks* is of interest with respect not only to genre (film noir, specifically) but also to performance. Drawing from sociologist Orrin E. Klapp, Richard Dyer has taught us that a star may personify a "social type," or "a shared, recognizable, easily grasped image of how people are in society (with collective approval or disapproval built into it)" (47). *Twin Peaks* is populated largely by US social types, even if some characters ultimately transcend, subvert, or at least problematize the types the series self-consciously deploys. As the previous chapter suggests, the "Independent Woman" emerges as the most recurring type, albeit mystified as the "femme fatale" through the patriarchal fears and desires the series lays bare. But there is also Kyle MacLachlan's "Good Joe," Dale Cooper; Dana Ashbrook's "Tough Guy," Bobby Briggs; and James Marshall's "Rebel," James Hurley, among others. This chapter considers the underexamined relationship between acting and character in *Twin Peaks*, focusing on three key roles: MacLachlan as Cooper, the Zen FBI special agent from Philadelphia assigned to investigate the murder of high school homecoming queen Laura Palmer; Ray Wise as respected attorney Leland Palmer, Laura's father, who murders her under the control of the inhabiting spirit BOB, played by Frank Silva; and Sheryl Lee as Laura, a victim of Leland/BOB's sexual abuse since the age of twelve. Although only glimpsed in the series through flashbacks and Red Room sequences, Laura is the protagonist of the feature film prequel *Twin Peaks: Fire Walk with Me*. We contend that these performances derive from the intersections of a modernist fragmentation and a melodramatic affect, constituting both the distinctive "strangeness" of the *Peaks* universe and its earnest appeals to pathos and emotion.

A unifying mode of address through acting would be difficult to establish here, especially given Lynch's caginess in interviews about his directorial methods and intentions. Moreover, cast members relied on heterogeneous styles, came from various backgrounds, carried different star images, and worked with multiple directors throughout the series (to say nothing of the gap between *Twin Peaks* and *The Return* that brought new actors to the series and asked older stars to reprise their roles after twenty-six years). Andreas Halskov comments on the unusual amount of freedom and control Lynch enjoyed in casting *Twin Peaks*, "using mainly his intuition and his sense of the visual (how a given actor would *look* on screen)" (64). Lynch "signed actors to nonscripted roles or based on loose ideas he had" (67–68), sometimes inspired by only a head shot (e.g., Sherilyn Fenn as Audrey Horne) or an informal conversation instead of a traditional reading (e.g., James Marshall as James Hurley). Similar to his casting process, Lynch's work with actors is concerned neither with characters' "motivation and backstory" nor with "character development and consistency," as actor Richard Beymer attested in Lynch's direction of his performance as Ben Horne (68).

Our concerns lie in the individual performances that contribute to the structuring motif of "acting strangely"—demonic possession, doubling, reversed backward speech—and thematize performance across *Twin Peaks*, *Twin Peaks: Fire Walk with Me*, and *The Return*. The hyperconsciousness of performance, we argue, makes performance itself an important narrative through line and formal component at the level of the visual style.[15] Lest one forget that the metatheatrical space of the Red Room functions as a stage for revelations that both characters and audiences are invited to experience.[16] James Naremore has pointed out that the camera always creates a "performance frame," which "designates spectacle" and "can contain various kinds of performance," including people "as actors playing theatrical personages, as public figures playing theatrical versions of themselves, and as documentary evidence" (*Acting* 15). For the purposes of this chapter, we will confine our analysis to "acting," the term Naremore uses for "a special type of theatrical performance in which the persons held up for show have become agents in the narrative" (23). Indeed, a whole other chapter could be written on music and performance, from Julee Cruise's appearances at the Roadhouse to the parade of artists Lynch curated to play in *The Return*.[17]

Before proceeding further, definitions of "modernist" and "melodramatic" performance are in order. With "modernist" cinema, we are referring to the late modernism of post–World War II art cinema (see Chapter 1). We understand "modernist" film performance in this context, as Robert T. Self defines it, "not to ultimately convey some sense of an 'individual' 'identity' but to portray personality as a subjectivity proscribed by contradictory forces. Thus, acting in modernist discourse works inevitably in the service of the depiction of splintered, unstable, and insecure identity" (127). Modernist cinema rejects the "unified social identity" and "autonomous individual" of classical cinema, which upholds characters as intelligible, as capable of ethical, meaningful action (127), and instead seeks "to represent a truer reality" through "'people,' not 'characters'" (128).

This definition only partly applies to *Twin Peaks*, which favors characters and performance based in social types (not ordinary social reality), while opting for the excesses and exaggerations of melodrama over the "dispassionate and detached voice" of modernism (Self 127). Recall from Chapter 2 that film melodrama grew out of nineteenth-century theater. In a short article on the performance styles in *Twin Peaks*, Stephen Lacey observes that melodrama necessitated "an acting style that was externalized and physicalized" to articulate "extreme emotional states" that the actor could hold long enough for the intensity and expressivity of emotion to register fully with the audience (128). Wise, MacLachlan, and Lee deliver performances that tacitly assert an aesthetic and philosophical project of modernism, questioning the efficacy of traditional linguistic communication and the idea of a self that exists outside of contradiction or division. Despite reflexivity and artifice that align *Twin Peaks* texts with modernist experimentation and innovation, the performances of suffering, existential uncertainty, and sexual trauma afford opportunities for what Bruce McConachie calls "gaining knowledge through feeling," a historical and affective tradition of melodrama (qtd. in Lacey 128). *Twin Peaks*, in the final analysis, presents models for Cooper's vision of "looking at the world with love" (Episode 18), while exploring Major Briggs's fear of "the possibility that love is not enough" (Episode 27).

Ray Wise/Leland Palmer

A scene in *Twin Peaks: Fire Walk with Me* encapsulates the modernist-melodramatic continuum on which we see these three actors. Leland has secretly responded to an advertisement in the swingers magazine *Flesh World* and just had sex with Teresa Banks, a seventeen-year-old diner waitress outside the town of Twin Peaks, who moonlights as a prostitute to support her cocaine addiction. Lying on top of her in their motel bed, he presses his hand over her eyes and asks, "Who am I?" Although clearly uncomfortable, Teresa seems to think Leland is using his hand as a blindfold to be kinky. Meanwhile, the audience knows he is wrestling with BOB's gradual influence and losing any sense of himself as BOB continues taking over. Teresa, who sometimes "parties" with Laura, will later become Leland/BOB's first victim when she discovers that Leland is Laura's father and attempts to blackmail him. Echoing Leland's question, Laura will later ask, "Who *are* you?" first as she sees electrical flickers on her bedroom ceiling, indicating BOB's presence, and again when BOB rapes her and reveals himself as Leland.

Twin Peaks: Fire Walk with Me attributes Leland's psychological duality to a supernatural cause (i.e., demonic possession), but this evil made manifest also has metaphorical significance as a monster from the id. BOB can be read as a psychological displacement of an incest victim unable to accept "the man behind the mask," the name Mrs. Tremond's grandson gives Leland, as her perpetrator (in Episode 14, Cooper learns that she referred to him as "a friend of her father's" in her secret diary).[18] The recurring image of the "phallic papier-mâché mask" (Nieland 88) extends this theatrical metaphor. Yet, BOB also represents the dark side of a father's psyche. After the film's release, according to Chris Rodley's interview book, Lynch "received many letters from young girls who had been abused by their fathers. [. . .] Despite the fact that the perpetration of both incest and filicide was represented in the 'abstract' form of Killer Bob, it was recognized as faithful to the subjective experience" (xii). There are times when Wise's performance gives Leland a fair amount of ambiguity, leaving audiences to wonder in those moments whether he is "all BOB," such as in the sex scene with Teresa Banks. Lynch believes the path to human enlightenment is attainable through negotiating the opposites that comprise the world, including psychic opposites in oneself; in order to appreciate the "light," one has to confront the "dark." What Lynch describes is not so much the conservative Manichean binary that gives melodrama its moral legibility but contradictory forces that remain coterminous in nature (Rodley 23). About *Twin Peaks: Fire Walk with Me*, he has said, "Laura's one of many people. It's her take on that. That's what it was all about—the loneliness, shame, guilt, confusion and devastation of the victim of incest. It also dealt with the torment of the father—the war in him" (185).

Leland, too, is a victim of abuse. In Episode 10, he identifies BOB as a man named Robertson who lived next door to his grandfather's summer house, where he vacationed with his family as a child, and in Episode 16 he admits that BOB would visit him in "dreams." The story Leland tells evokes the repressed memories of a rape: "He said he wanted to play. He opened me and I invited him and he came inside me." The "war" in Leland to which Lynch refers is acted out on both diegetic and metadiegetic levels of performance. As BOB's human vessel, Leland is forced to embody him and enact his unthinkable crimes (screaming, "don't make me do this!" before murdering Laura).

Throughout *Twin Peaks*, Leland's episodes of singing and dancing literalize BOB's "performance." Perhaps not coincidentally, Leland Palmer is also the name of a Broadway performer who starred in musicals during the 1960s and 1970s (Kalinak 86). Mocking Leland's grief over the loss of his daughter, BOB has him play a recording of the jazz standard "Pennsylvania 6–5000" and dance while clutching Laura's portrait ("we have to dance," he tells Sarah after wailing hysterically) (Episode 2). Following Laura's funeral, he tearfully begs guests at the Great Northern to dance with him, a kind of perverse variation on the *Danse Macabre* (Episode 3), and later breaks into another dancing-crying fit in front of Ben Horne's investors from Iceland (Episode 5). As BOB's influence strengthens in the second season, signaled by Leland's hair turning white, Leland erupts into renditions of old pop songs and show tunes ("Mairzy Doats," "Get Happy," "Getting to Know You"), purporting to show his final acceptance of Laura's death when actually revealing BOB's delight in getting away with murder.

Frost and Lynch finally "unmask" BOB in Episode 14, although they always knew it would be Leland (Rodley 181). To conceal the twist from the cast and crew until just before this

63

episode aired, Lynch went so far as to shoot two different versions (one with Leland killing Maddy Ferguson and one with Ben Horne as the murderer), and both were edited, mixed, and color corrected. Wise was heartbroken when Frost and Lynch informed him that the episode would reveal Leland as Laura's murderer ("Secrets"). The camera shows BOB's reflection in the mirror looking back at Leland, who, in another meta-theatrical moment, has straightened his tie and turns behind him, breaking the "fourth wall" by looking into the camera (the sounds of a phonograph needle over the trail-off groove of a record produce a tense, heartbeat rhythm). Leland/BOB's murder of Maddy, illuminated by a spotlight, will become a harrowing, dance-like "show," and BOB must get into character before showtime. When Leland disposes of Maddy's corpse in Episode 15, he sings "The Surrey with the Fringe on Top" from Rodgers and Hammerstein's *Oklahoma!* (1943) with wicked glee, and only in his last dying moments does he regain his soul after BOB departs (Episode 16).

Prior to his role on *Twin Peaks*, Wise was best known for playing attorney Jamie Rawlins on the long-running daytime soap opera *Love of Life* (CBS, 1951–80) between 1970 and 1976, and he had recurring roles throughout the 1980s on prime-time soaps, including *Dallas*, *Knots Landing* (CBS, 1979–93), and *The Colbys* (ABC, 1985–87). The acting demands of *Twin Peaks* required Wise to operate on a whole other level of television melodrama. In his foundational book on David Lynch, Michel Chion argues that "Lynch dared to make his actors sob, running the risk of stifling the symmetrical effect of tears among the spectators" (115). With the "welling up of tears, like a slow constriction," Chion explains, the actor "alters and convulses the face," which then "contorts and becomes ugly" (115).

Twin Peaks couples such heightened emotion with "a non-psychological and non-naturalistic logic of roles" (Chion 109) in "a world of archetypes" (111), such as the social and generic types mentioned earlier. Chion claims that characters run

Ray Wise as Leland Palmer, reflected as BOB (*Twin Peaks*, Episode 14).

"true to type" or "acquire a mythical quality" (e.g., BOB, MIKE, the Chalfonts/Tremonds, The Arm/Man from Another Place, The Fireman/Giant) (107, 109). Another category consists of characters "singled out by some physical aspect of their appearance, such as a piece of clothing or favorite accessory which is semantically associated with them" (e.g., Audrey Horne's sensual dancing and posing, Gordon Cole's hearing aid, Leland's white hair) (107–8). We would add that Wise's grimacing facial expressions and compulsive dancing define his character by providing the visible "language" of pantomime for Leland's experience of despair and conflict, a modernist crisis of epistemology and identity ("Who am I?") that exceeds linguistic communication. Taking Chion's thesis further, we could think of most characters in *Twin Peaks* as "actors," in that they are defined by hair, makeup, costume, movement, gesture, and behavior. They are "non-psychological" and therefore require the external and physical acting conventions of melodrama to signify as characters. However, they do not lack the complex, deeply layered subjectivities associated with modernist representation.

What makes Wise's performance astonishing is how he convincingly juxtaposes emotions (crying and dancing) and characters (Leland and BOB) within a single scene. Wise's code-shifting between Leland and BOB establishes a performance vocabulary that often but not always allows the audience to distinguish the characters from each other (warm smile, polite manner, and overwrought agony for Leland; scowls and evil grins, manic energy and intensity, and raspy voice for BOB). Consider the scene in *Twin Peaks: Fire Walk with Me* when Wise sits hunched on the edge of Leland's bed, rocking back and forth with his head tilted down, mouth curled in a grin, and eyes staring slightly up from under his eyebrows. Suddenly, his grin melts and his eyes soften; his face trembles as he begins to weep. It is clear that Leland remembers sadistically reprimanding Laura earlier in the evening (as BOB) for sitting down to dinner with "filthy" hands (a veiled and jealous condemnation of her sexual activity). Leland's pain and sorrow only provide sustenance for BOB, ensuring that this transformation is temporary, and his powerlessness imbues the scene with the pathos of melodramatic irreversibility. Audiences of *Twin Peaks* already know both Leland's and Laura's tragic fates.

Kyle MacLachlan/Dale Cooper

Whereas Wise's performance holds in tension two selves occupying the same body, MacLachlan plays a character who splits into two different bodies: the "Good Joe" Cooper and his "shadow self" from the Black Lodge, who merges with BOB in the Season 2 finale and goes by the nickname "Mr. C" in *The Return*. MacLachlan rose to stardom with Lynch's *Blue*

Velvet and his earlier *Dune* (1984), an adaptation of the classic 1965 science-fiction novel by Frank Herbert that flopped both critically and commercially. In 1987, he also starred in a science-fiction action-thriller called *The Hidden*, playing an extraterrestrial masquerading as an FBI agent. With *Twin Peaks* and *The Return*, he demonstrated an extraordinary acting range into which previous films and television series had not fully tapped.

Fans of *Twin Peaks* will fondly remember MacLachlan's sensitivity and boyish charm as Cooper, his enthusiastic "thumbs up" signs and outpourings of excitement over doughnuts, cherry pie, and hot black coffee ("damn good coffee" quickly became a shibboleth of *Peaks* fandom). Cooper's wonder in discovering the majestic beauty of Douglas firs, his fulfillment by simple culinary pleasures, and his obsession with tape-recording his detailed observations and interpretations of the day—ostensibly for the benefit of his secretary Diane—reflect an awe of and delighted curiosity in the natural world. The town of Twin Peaks abounds with mysteries to be investigated, organized, and *sensed* (seen, heard, smelled, tasted, and felt).

It is no surprise that his method of detection combines the logic and precision of deductive reasoning with the spirituality of Tibetan Buddhism, a belief in ethical principles and community values, and a receptivity to dreams, resulting in "a mind-body coordination operating hand-in-hand with the deepest level of intuition" (Episode 2). As Martha Nochimson asserts in her pioneering feminist analysis, Cooper's perceptive abilities are not without gendered implications for *Twin Peaks* as a detective series. If the "Hollywood Mystery Tradition" equates femininity with the unknowable and therefore the dangerous, traditional masculine detective heroes must transfer their fears of vulnerability onto women's bodies (sexualized femmes fatales or desexualized murder victims) and take recourse in the narrow, culturally determined "facts" of reality (144–45). By contrast, Nochimson argues, Cooper does not disavow the feminine to restore phallocentric clarity, but rather seeks to "move between masculinity and femininity" to solve the mystery of Laura's murder with an open mind (151).

When a dream transports Cooper to the Red Room twenty-five years in the future at the end of Episode 2, Laura whispers the identity of her murderer in his ear and "seals" her message with a kiss. "Better to listen than to talk," the Giant later admonishes. In effect, Laura solves the mystery for Cooper at the beginning of the series (Nochimson 151); she is "neither a sexualized or desexualized object," but rather a subject in her own murder mystery (152). Nochimson points out how Cooper "gains knowledge through merging with her" and the pleasure of her kiss compounds the satisfaction of their mutual desires: his to understand and hers to communicate (152). Over the first fifteen episodes, Cooper must learn to "'hear' Laura with his conscious mind" (151) and remember her words, as surrounding patriarchal figures of Twin Peaks consistently fail to guarantee authority (150). The Laura Palmer case leads Cooper to seismic uncertainty, but by relinquishing control, he also liberates himself from fear and undertakes a different hero's journey, one of human compassion and connection.

Lean, square-jawed, and clean-shaven, with his almost permanently slicked-back hair, Cooper sort of resembles a superhero (uniformed in the Hollywood detective's beige trench coat, black suit, white shirt, and tie instead of tights and a cape). On the one hand, his fashion sense conveys his consummate professionalism, but on the other, it shows a comfort with the senses of those around him. Cooper does a great deal of looking in his investigation and he is also *looked at* himself, primarily by Audrey Horne, who motivates a structure of looking that positions Cooper on the receiving end of a desiring gaze. Conceived as his exact opposite, Mr. C appears as a grotesque parody of hypermasculinity: cowboy boots, a biker's black leather jacket, and a rock star's mane of wild, greasy hair. To say he lacks Cooper's sense of style would be an understatement.

Never relying on costumes or accessories exclusively, MacLachlan distinguishes Mr. C from Cooper in the way he walks and talks. The eager, wide-eyed Cooper strides through space (Chion 153), speaking with animated facial expressions and a "sing song" delivery. Conversely, Mr. C swaggers with macho bravado, his face resting in a disturbingly flat affect. Mr. C's monotone voice and clipped, matter-of-fact speech patterns betray a crudeness of thought, a lack of emotion, and an inability to feel, with a will to violence that supplants Cooper's wish "to treat people with much more care and respect" (Episode 8). Part 2, for example, contains an excruciating scene in which Mr. C lies in bed next to his criminal partner, Darya, who, he realizes, has double-crossed him. Ignoring her attempts to distract him with her body, he coldly attacks and then shoots her dead before proceeding to another motel room to have sex with a second female associate, Chantal. Although Chantal happily consents, the scene recapitulates the earlier moment of sexualized violence by equating sex with violence as bids for domination and control in the new world order of *Twin Peaks*. *The Return* announces to audiences that we are a long way from Cooper's interception of dream messages or Leland's desperate struggle to overcome BOB, and that for all of our nostalgia, it will be impossible to return to Twin Peaks as we remember it.

Throughout most of *The Return*, the "good Dale" exists in an amnesiac, near-catatonic state after escaping the Red Room in Part 2, taking the place of a Las Vegas insurance agent named Dougie Jones (a Cooper clone whom Mr. C created at one point as a decoy). MacLachlan does not so much play a new version of Cooper as allow him to restore his sensorial mode of engagement (gently touching objects with bemusement, shuffling his feet as if having just learned to walk, blinking slowly as if processing the immensity of the visual field, repeating the last word or phrase said to him in an attempt to speak by listening). Good deeds are instinctual for Dougie, just as they are instinctually understood without traditional means of language; he exposes links to organized crime and police corruption in his insurance agency by doodling on case files. The sleeper awakens only through the call of duty and call to justice, the experience of romantic and familial love, and the familiar taste of coffee and pie.

Sheryl Lee/Laura Palmer

Cooper's cathartic awakening in Part 16 is not the first time *Twin Peaks* revived one of its characters. "At the end of the [1990–91] series," Lynch said, "I felt sad. I couldn't get myself to leave the world of Twin Peaks. I was in love with the character of Laura Palmer and her contradictions: radiant on the surface but dying inside. I wanted to see her live, move and talk" (Rodley 184). A profoundly empathetic and misunderstood film, *Twin Peaks: Fire Walk with Me* allowed Lynch to tell Laura's story, at last, from her own perspective. Chion calls it "a truly generous project because it delves into a character who, after her death, serves everyone as a prop for their own projections and fantasies, in order to say: this character existed and suffered—take an interest in this woman" (145). Focusing on the last days of Laura's life before her murder, the film took a much darker and more experimental approach than the series, deemphasizing its folksy humor and refusing to answer questions left hanging by the Season 2 finale. Audiences at Cannes allegedly booed its premiere (Lynch and McKenna 310), and it vacated theaters in most countries practically two weeks after it opened, receiving especially harsh reviews in the US (Lucas 29). The press dismissed it as Lynch's cynical attempt to exploit the former popularity of a canceled television series (Rodley 184), but the film nevertheless has ardent defenders—more and more in the years since its release. Writing about Lee, the critic Greil Marcus trumpeted, "The film is driven by as heedless a performance as any in the history of film" (147).

A stage actor working in Seattle, Lee was an unknown on television and film prior to *Twin Peaks*. Lynch and Frost cast her to play Laura's bluish-gray corpse wrapped in plastic, as they were shooting the pilot outside of Seattle, but later created the part of Maddy for her on the basis of a "presence and a natural ability" Lynch noticed in the video footage shot for the taped picnic that Cooper studies in the pilot (Rodley 174). The character of Maddy, Laura's twin cousin introduced in Episode 3, was important to the narrative arc of the first fourteen episodes (another instance of *Peaks*ian doubling). However, Laura remains the most iconic character of the series, an image framed in a photograph, ubiquitous in her visibility but never legible to the town outside of a type: either the blonde, blue-eyed "good girl" (the all-American feminine ideal) or the "femme fatale" (a good girl gone bad, a moralistic cautionary tale). Ignoring or denying her suffering, the town cast her in a "double role" that rendered her inscrutable as a person, while in death she returns as an oracle of the Red Room uttering obscure clues in reversed backward speech that only the most attuned can decipher.

Twin Peaks: Fire Walk with Me granted Lee the opportunity to "move and talk" as Laura with a performance that demystifies her status as the image of a passive victim, an object frozen in time and memory, reconstituting Laura as a feeling subject and the most affectively responsive character in *Twin Peaks*. Lee constantly referred to Jennifer Lynch's *The Secret Diary of Laura Palmer* to access the character's psychology and experiences and help shape performance decisions (Hallam, *Twin Peaks* 104–5). For Lynch, as Justus Nieland brilliantly illuminates, melodrama and modernism are not mutually exclusive. Melodrama is "a basic category of modern experience" and its characters are "radio-active," or "receivers and transmitters in a mediated network of affect and action" (81), an apt metaphor given Hollywood melodrama's association with the built environment and media ecology of the Atomic Age home. To whatever degree *Twin Peaks: Fire Walk with Me* relies on modernist estrangement or an ironizing of domestic melodrama, Nieland insists that it still "depends on melodrama's long-standing capacity to respond—through affect—to larger crises in social value, signification, and significance." It is "modernist melodrama" (82). Lee's performance alternates between "big" emotion and quieter, more contemplative expressions, positioning Laura as a conduit between Leland/BOB and Cooper in a circuit of affective energies. In enduring Leland/BOB's abuse and allowing him to murder her instead of giving him possession of her body, a decision symbolized by her acceptance of the jade green ring from the Red Room, Laura passes on to that liminal space where she is able to help Cooper crack the case and ultimately free Leland from BOB at the end of Episode 16. Were BOB to possess Laura successfully, he would presumably empower the "extreme negative force" in the universe known as "Judy."

Similar to Wise in *Twin Peaks*, Lee expresses suffering through tears and sobs, often using her entire body. She quivers violently or gasps for air in scenes when she realizes that BOB is in fact Leland, opening her mouth as if to let out a scream that never manages to leave her throat. Elsewhere, she does scream. Few characters in twentieth- and twenty-first-century popular culture are more linked to an actor's scream than Laura Palmer. *Twin Peaks* introduced the "Laura scream" in a brief flashback to her murder at the end of Episode 8, a visceral counterpoint to the breathy voice Lee adopts for Laura in Dr. Jacoby's tapes and other flashbacks (Laura is clearly "playing a role" there). An expression of terror then becomes a means of terrorizing in Episode 29 when Laura's doppelganger twists her mouth open and generates reversed backward screams in the Red Room. Laura's screams in *Twin Peaks: Fire Walk with Me* are such that the screams themselves seem painful, both for the sheer force of her voice and way Lee stretches her mouth to an unnaturally wide gape. Finally, the last scene of Part 18 in *The Return* ends with a scream that echoes into the night, crossing both temporal and generational boundaries. Cooper and Laura have been revived yet again, this time as somnambulant new characters Richard and Carrie, respectively, throwing the series into further ontological confusion. Visiting the Palmer house triggers Carrie's memories of the trauma in her past life, the site of *Twin Peaks's* eternal return that cannot be rewritten.

Lee is perhaps most impressive, though, when she holds her body in steady composure, draining her face of recognizable emotions from easily identifiable causes. Before prostituting herself at the Roadhouse, she encounters two women who nearly bring her to tears. First, the Log Lady approaches her in the parking lot and touches her face, then her hand, and Laura stares at a reflection of herself in the window and deliberates the Log Lady's concerned, poetic warning. Second, when Laura enters the bar and sees Julee Cruise on stage singing "Questions in a World of Blue," her angelic voice and lyrics about sadness and loss seize Laura in melancholy identification. Both women seem to have been able to "hear" her, as Cooper learns to do and as others cannot. Laura takes some comfort in her companionship with her best friend Donna, but even Donna seems able to relate to her only in terms of adolescent romances (gushing over Laura's "sweet" and "gorgeous" secret boyfriend

Sheryl Lee (*left*) as Laura Palmer and Kyle MacLachlan (*right*) as Dale Cooper in *Twin Peaks: Fire Walk with Me* (David Lynch, 1992).

James). Reclining upside down in a living room chair, her feet dangling over the backrest and her head lying on the footrest, Laura describes to Donna "falling faster and faster" into a void, not feeling anything until "bursting into fire forever." More than the melodrama of tears or terrified screams, Lee opens a new dimension in *Twin Peaks* by personifying, once again, that melodramatic question, "what if?" (see Chapter 2). What if it were possible to live in a world where the angels haven't "all gone away," as she mournfully concludes in her living room daydream with Donna? What if it is possible to feel the hand of another person, and to be touched by a performance?

Peaks Paratexts

Adaptation, Remediation, and Transmedia Storytelling

In Part 13 of *The Return*, Walter, the corporate rep negotiating a franchise of the Double R Diner, tells Norma that her "home" restaurant is not as profitable as the newer ones in the franchise. Norma contends that customers have complained that the pies she is known for aren't as good at the other diners, to which Walter advises an "artistic compromise," that Norma revise her recipes in accord with the pies sold at the other Double Rs. Walter's comment, that there is need for "tweaking the formula to ensure consistency and profitability," speaks to Frost and Lynch's ambivalence about the idea of *Twin Peaks* becoming a franchise, this anxiety reflecting the creators' desire to maintain artistic control over *The Return* within the context of corporate hierarchies. The art-of-pies metaphor gains strength when we consider the show's repeated association of pie with pleasure, and further, survival, as the cherry pie Dougie brings to the Mitchum brothers in the desert in Part 11 of *The Return* saves his life.

In perhaps a fairly obvious sense, the "evil" associated with doppelgangers in *The Return* similarly functions as a critique of imitation and copying—assaults on the originality and uniqueness of individual identity. The ethics of uniqueness is most prominently associated with the Log Lady, whose special "kind of knowing" Robert Jacoby (the psychiatrist's brother) pays tribute to in *The Secret History of Twin Peaks* (Frost 2016, henceforth *The Secret History*). "With difference comes misunderstanding" (315), says Jacoby—meaning, in the spirit of *Twin Peaks*, that embracing what is different or other is a challenging task in which the universe of *Twin Peaks* is thoroughly invested. So, how different can *The Return* be from its previous iteration and still attract an audience and compel viewers familiar with the series who desire, like the Odyssean Cooper at the end of *The Return*, to go back to their "home text" (Grossman, *Literature* 12)? Frost and Lynch understand the tightrope walk involved in maintaining the same tone and characters that earlier drew viewers to *Twin Peaks* while at the same time needing to avoid a formulaic "return," adapting the stories and characters to varied contexts and a different socio-cultural-historical moment.

Certainly, the worlds of *Twin Peaks* provide comfort in sameness: a joyful frisson in hearing Angelo Badalamenti's score begin again after it is withheld for the first two minutes of *The Return*; a pleasurable sense of stability in knowing in 2017 that Andy and Lucy are still wise and sometimes courageous fools and that FBI agent Albert Rosenfield maintains his irony and barbed sense of humor; gratification in learning that although Sheriff Harry Truman is absent (and sick with cancer), his brother, Sheriff Frank Truman, remains, as the Log Lady says, a "true man"; delight in seeing, in Las Vegas, that Cooper's traits "will out" ("coff-eee") and relief that, in the end, "Cooper, the one and only" (as Diane calls him in Part 17) will awaken from his catatonic state encased within the life of Dougie Jones. In giving us substantial elements of character and story patterns we remember from the early 1990s, Frost and Lynch do provide the benefits of franchise, the "institutionally-based demands for 'more' and 'further'" that comprise the energy of reboots in popular entertainment properties (Palmer 77).

And yet from the beginning *Twin Peaks* has resisted ame-
liorative nostalgia. It is the case that in Seasons 1 and 2, Frost
and Lynch have transplanted 1950s styles into a present-day
setting. A postmodern interpretation could attribute this decision to a nostalgia for an idealized past that removes it from its
historical conditions and specificity (see Ramsay and Lafky),
but Frost has explained that a kind of timelessness *does* exist in
many small towns in the US, the reality of which motivated a
setting where "time has kind of stood still for a while" (at least
for twenty or thirty years) ("Mark Frost"). Many of Lynch's films
take place in similar retro-1950s worlds, but he sees the world
of his characters reflecting that of his audience, where recycled
postwar culture (oldies stations, television reruns) creates "opportunities to re-live the past" (Rodley 278). What Lynch describes is less a retreat into myth or a longing for a perpetual
present than the hyperconsciousness of cultural memory and
time's passing. "There is some kind of present," he has said,
"but the present is the most elusive because it's going real fast"
(Rodley 278).

   The Return underscores Frost and Lynch's adaptation of the
small-town setting to call attention to the passage of time but
also the dangers embedded in tranquility. The town has generated its own "Dweller on the Threshold," the aspects of character Frost identifies in *Twin Peaks: The Final Dossier* (henceforth
The Final Dossier) as "the sum total of all the dark, negative,
unresolved qualities that reside in every human being" (11). It
isn't just that within the story tulpas melodramatically disrupt
"normal" life in *The Return*. In some ways more disturbing in
the show's reprise is the menace of a looming stasis and the
consequent anxiety that indeed very little has changed. This
threat of quietude is anatomized in *The Return*, where many
of the characters remain fixed in their forms from twenty-five
years earlier: Lucy is bewildered by cellular phone technology;
James is still pining romantically for a woman (Renee)—or the
idea of a woman—he can't have; Shelly is again involved with a

Sheryl Lee as Carrie Page, back "home" in the final moments (*The Return*, Part 18).

wrong guy (and her daughter, Becky, has embarked on the same path with her abusive husband, Steven); and even when Laura is not Laura (Carrie Page), she is still drawn fatally back to *being* Laura, as her final scream demonstrates.

The traps laid within the story worlds of *Twin Peaks* are set to capture characters within fixed positions, such immobility becoming one source of women wishing desperately to break out of their received roles, as discussed in Chapter 3. Add to this sense of confinement the presence in 2017 of drugs, young agitated addicts at the Roadhouse reflecting the pervasive severity of the contemporary opioid epidemic. Drug-addled Steven seems to have committed suicide after a painful exchange with a suffering Gersten Hayward (Donna's sister), who, we are told in *The Final Dossier*, had struggled with mental-health issues and "turned to stronger street drugs for comfort, concurrent with the nationwide trend in dependence on opioids and designer synthetics" (27).

The inertia and lethal traps in which characters are caught are further reflected in a material corrosion besetting the town. Unexplained instances of decay abound: the decomposing face of a jail dweller; a young, jittery woman scratching the rash under her arm at the Roadhouse; a deathly ill girl vomiting ghastly fluids, who sits in a car beside a hysterical woman trapped in a traffic jam—this follows a shooting incident where a sullen, defiant boy tries to emulate his equally creepy father by shooting a gun at the Double R. These grotesqueries define a rotting town. Frost has made clear, as referenced in Chapters 2 and 3, that the world of 2017 isn't the same Twin Peaks, whose denizens must confront the atrophy and rottenness associated with trying to hold onto a world that no longer exists, a world yearning to maintain its "Special Agents" as stable and restorative figures—and, of course, that world wasn't very good in the first place, as the frog-moth creature and horrifying White Sands sequence in Part 8 amply show.

We already knew that darkness was an integral part of Twin Peaks, culminating at the end of Season 2 when Cooper's doppelganger merges with BOB. How is it possible, *Twin Peaks* asks, to adapt to change without going "nuclear," without carrying with you a ferocious violence? In some sense, the stories of *Twin Peaks* that exist beyond the boundaries of the original series suggest a negotiation between fixity and destructive disruption: it is the imaginative energy of *Twin Peaks*'s continuations—its paratexts and *The Return*—that are pitched against the forces of sameness and violation that threaten both the diegetic and the nondiegetic elements of this universe.

A creative rejoinder to fixity, the dynamism that characterizes the permeable fictional contours of the universe of *Twin Peaks* works to resist categorization. We see this most readily in debates about *The Return*'s status as cinema or television referenced in Chapter 1. In this vein, the Showtime event's incorporation of high-art tone and pace—extended silences that pepper the dialogue—and long takes and surrealist visuals destabilize the medium when elements of the show are paradoxically "hypermedial," making us aware of their artistic intent, and also "realistic" in an effort to capture the awkward and weird small moments of daily life (as Laura Dern said about *The Return*, "David [Lynch] doesn't abandon his characters when they're not doing something big" [Lynch and McKenna 489]).

As against stasis, and sameness, or nefarious imitation (Mr. C) and commercial exploitation (ensuring "consistency" of the brand), the pleasure of a particularly good cherry pie stands alongside characters, stories, and visual images that are distinct, unique, or different. And indeed, the effect of extending the world of *Twin Peaks* in its paratexts is to resist reification of *Twin Peaks*, the idea that it is one stable thing. And so we have been introduced to paratexts written by an extended authorial family: *Welcome to Twin Peaks: Access Guide to the Town* (1991); collectible trading cards; Lynch-directed commercials for Georgia Coffee that aired in Japan; Lynch's prequel film *Twin Peaks: Fire Walk with Me* (henceforth *Fire Walk with Me*); Jennifer Lynch's *The Secret Diary of Laura Palmer* (henceforth *The Secret Diary*); soundtrack albums; the audiobook (recorded by Kyle MacLaghlan) *"Diane . . .": The Twin Peaks Tapes of Agent Cooper* and novel *The Autobiography of F.B.I. Special Agent Dale Cooper: My Life, My Tapes* (henceforth *The Autobiography*), both written by Mark Frost's brother Scott; an official fan-club magazine called the *Twin Peaks Gazette*, canceled after three issues in conjunction with the series cancellation in 1991; and Mark Frost's *The Secret History* and *The Final Dossier*.

The intermedial storytelling of "Twin Peaks" blurs boundaries and resists closure, implying an ethics of world building pitched against objectification in all of its forms, in the identities of selves and texts. *Twin Peaks* argues for "open borders," whether this be redefining a medium or resisting the categorization of humans, especially women, as things or types, as we saw in Chapter 3. *Twin Peaks* paratexts continually redraw the contours and "maps" of their fictional places, pushing beyond the story's initial boundaries. Such movement and vitality are, in the end, the organizing principles of the universe, as indeed electricity becomes an increasingly central trope in *The Return*.

Twin Peaks exemplifies major "electrical currents" in contemporary intermedial storytelling. These have been theorized with varying points of focus: (1) remediation, where stories appearing in different media paradoxically bring readers closer to the fictional worlds they represent, while at the same time call attention to the act of mediation (see Bolter and Grusin); (2) transmedia, following Henry Jenkins's groundbreaking studies of storytelling across media platforms, thus creating elements of a fictional world that converge intermedially; (3) remakes, sequels, trilogies, reboots, and franchises, where a text or series will "co-exist" with or reinterpret a known set of characters and stories (see Verevis); and (4) adaptation studies in general, which may incorporate the previous models of textual reprise, emphasizing the multiple ways in which adaptive revisitations provide "repetition with variation" (Hutcheon 4). These ways of conceiving of textual production and reception not only create a path for understanding *Twin Peaks*'s singular and representative role but also suggest the show's helpfulness in further clarifying the place of adaptive modes of storytelling in contemporary culture and society. R. Barton Palmer recently observed that "all texts are fragments in the sense that they await gestures of continuation that challenge the mirage of self-containment in which they are mistakenly thought to endure" (76).

There is hardly a better example of this adaptive model of textuality than *Twin Peaks*'s intimate conversation among its texts and paratexts. Indeed, *Twin Peaks* demonstrates the work of textual continuation to question where texts begin and end, like the Log Lady's reflection on death as "just a change, not an end" in Part 15 (or MIKE's question to Cooper in the Red Room, "is it future or is it past?"). The show interrogates fixed and fluid human and textual identities, offering a generative model of textuality, or "elasTEXTity" (see Grossman, *Literature*) that posits story worlds as open and unceasing.

If, in 1995, David Lavery called *Twin Peaks* a "completely furnished world" ("Introduction" 7), the abundance of story and affect associated with this fictional universe is also due to its susceptibility to *more* furnishings, an expansion of its world by extension and paratext. At first blush there are pleasures aplenty in what Thomas Leitch aptly describes (drawing from Wolfgang Iser) as the gaps that are created and filled by adaptations (see "Mind the Gaps"). *Twin Peaks* paratexts delight in filling gaps, telling us (in the Twin Peaks guidebook), for example, that visitors no less diverse and luminary than Oscar Wilde (in 1902), Enrico Caruso (in 1918), and The Guess Who (in 1969) have appeared or performed in the town. We learn that Jerry Horne's favorite restaurant in Twin Peaks is Angelo Wong's Italian-Thai restaurant. In *The Autobiography*, we discover that young Dale sent letters not only to J. Edgar Hoover but also to Efrem Zimbalist Jr., star of the television series *The F.B.I.* (1965–74); we also find out that Dale scored 800 on his English and Math SATs (70). Later, when Cooper first meets Diane on December 17, 1977, he describes her as "an interesting cross between a saint and a cabaret singer" (Scott Frost, *Autobiography* 147). In *The Secret History*, we learn that James Hurley's favorite book is *Charlotte's Web* (1952) and Andy's *The World According to Garp* (1978). We see the postcard that Norma sent to her parents in the spring of 1969 on her honeymoon with Hank Jennings, brimming with joy at having seen a taping of *The Tonight Show* with guests Sammy Davis Jr. and Victor Buono. With multitextual and multitextural fervor, *The Secret History* recounts meticulously the secret history of Doug Milford, journalist ex-military brother of Mayor Duane Milford: Doug had close connections to the mysteries of Roswell and extraterrestrial happenings throughout the postwar US, culminating in meetings with President Nixon and Jackie Gleason (giving new meaning, as Special Agent Tammy Preston notes in the margins of these reports, to the phrase "to the moon, Alice!" [296]).

Such wild juxtapositions satisfy our curiosity with imaginative blends of popular culture and political history. But they also create an uncanny convergence of the "likely" and the "unlikely" that enhance and direct the fictional world toward something more closely related to our real experiences. After all, as

Lynch told Chris Rodley after the initial series ended, "Twin Peaks is still there, it's just that no one is pointing the camera at it now" (Rodley 181). On the one hand, the *Twin Peaks* story world invites an exhaustive filling in that produces the illusion of completion; on the other hand, such filling in could be, in theory and perhaps actually, endless.

Resisting closure and objectification of its own stories and characters, these paratexts have a more serious purpose than engaging our delight in their creative energy. They function to challenge our preconceived notions about stories, characters, and their worlds and to prod us to reconsider and reevaluate our interpretations of texts and worlds we think we know. So it is that in *The Final Dossier*, Frost fills the gaps in Annie Smith Blackburn's sad story, or weighs in further on Josie as a femme fatale, to return to an idea in Chapter 3. Frost alludes to *Body Heat* (1981) twice and calls Josie Packard a "dangerous sociopath" (99); he had earlier drawn out the lethal elements of the character in *The Secret History*, saying that she was "smart as a snake" (13). And yet, the performance by Joan Chen complicates such simple abstraction of Josie into a type. It is worth noting that in 1991, *Twin Peaks* earned a "Jimmie" award from the Association of Asian/Pacific American Artists (named after celebrated cinematographer James Wong Howe) for casting Joan Chen in a role that wasn't originally conceived as Asian. Isabella Rossellini was initially supposed to play Giovanna Packard, but when she dropped out of the project, the role was reconceived as "Josie Packard," with Chen cast in the part, supporting the idea that "talented actors of any color can play almost any role if simply given the opportunity" (Tusher 18). Frost may later refer to Josie as a "sociopath," but the performance by Chen, as well as Catherine's surprising empathy toward her nemesis after Josie has died, unsettles easy categorization (Frost himself notes in *The Secret History* that part of what motivates Catherine's re-clusiveness after the fire that kills Pete Martell is the loss of her rival Josie, for whom she had developed a high regard and with whom she had formed a strong if complicated bond). These revisitations of story and character catalyze viewers' reception, conceptualization, and experience regarding them, as we toggle among representations to try to reassemble the puzzles of meaning offered to us. As Marie-Laure Ryan has said about transmedia stories, we "return to them over and over again, not to relive the same experience, but to make new discoveries" (539).

In some ways the ever-expanding fiction of *Twin Peaks* was anticipated by Frost and Lynch in their earliest conversations about the series, since they began their collaboration by drawing a map of the town. Establishing the story immediately as a concrete visual phenomenon, Frost and Lynch set the stage for the show's paratexts that further delineate the world. In September of 1990, *Twin Peaks* was just premiering its second season at the same time as David Lynch's daughter Jennifer published *The Secret Diary*. The novel sat in fourth place on the *New York Times* bestseller list, remediating the diary from the show on a different fictional platform and giving voice to the traumatized teenager at the absent center of *Twin Peaks*. *The Secret Diary* articulates Laura's "sad thoughts" (8), as she reveals the truth of her life, that she is a "darker person than the town thinks" (172). We knew this from the series, as bits of Laura's sorrowful story are revealed. But what is reinforced in this revelatory paratext is Laura's struggle—her rage ("such an anger" [71]) at BOB for victimizing her; her attempts at altruism, starting Twin Peaks's "Meals on Wheels" program and tutoring Josie and Johnny Horne; and her efforts to gain power by taking control of her sexuality and performing the role of femme fatale to assert some agency in a brutally difficult psychological and social setting. She says in the middle of the diary that she has no self-determination, asserting poetically that she was "born without a choice" (100). As against this rendering of her as victim, Laura engages in drugs and sex to escape her pain and to try to control her experience. We are not only brought inside

Laura's psychological devastation, empathizing with her vitality and her desolation, readers are given another perspective on the limits of a small and claustrophobic social world, where the "same faces" appear (31). Part of the challenge, that is—again, in particular for the women of *Twin Peaks*—is to deal with the fact of being "terribly bored."

As a remediated object of revelation, the diary brings to life a new perspective on Laura Palmer. It is worth noting that Sheryl Lee has helped to remediate further and give voice to Laura's story by narrating the diary in an audiobook. Such adaptations merge actors and texts via performance in a way that further realizes the idea put forth in Chapter 4 that performance exceeds the boundaries of diegetic character. In suggesting that story worlds are open and unceasing, the transmedial stories that constitute the *Twin Peaks* universe posit authorship, adaptation, and performance as mutually enhancing processes. In some sense, the paratexts themselves perform new roles for *Twin Peaks*.[19] Imagining *Twin Peaks* paratexts as "free agents," performing new iterations of the story world, conforms with Lynch's own remarks about the vitality of *Twin Peaks* (Lynch having said that he has, over time, wondered what the Twin Peaks folks were up to). He has thus cast himself and Frost as "receivers" who document what's happening in Twin Peaks, validating its presence, blurring the line between what's real and fictional, and transferring agency away from writer and director and toward the text itself. In this way, the paratexts may be seen as organically grown story-catalysts, reminding us of the energy and potential of source texts to shift and change, intermedially and temporally, into new forms, media, stories. After all, "the noun *adaptation*," writes Leitch, "is subordinate to the verb *adapt*" ("To Adapt or To Adapt To" 101).

Part of this agency of the text as it adapts and evolves (see Hutcheon and Bortolotti on a Darwinian view of adaptation) is the extent to which its paratexts shape our viewing of the entire experience of the story world. So it is with *Fire Walk with Me* that the absence of Laura Palmer in the series is remediated as powerful presence. *Fire Walk with Me* works in conversation with *The Secret Diary* to explore the subjective experience of Laura Palmer. Lee's performance poignantly demonstrates this character's traumas in the days before her death, Lynch commenting on his motive for making the film, "I wanted to go back and see what she was going through during those days before she died" (Lynch and McKenna 324). The film mystified and frustrated initial audiences, illustrating the sometimes neuralgic experience for audiences of seeing their known texts reimagined and re-presented by paratexts or adaptations. Writing in the *New York Times*, Vincent Canby, for example, declared, "It's not the worst movie ever made; it just seems to be" (11). As Michel Chion reports, "Lynch was accused of playing the spoiled auteur who thinks he can get away with anything, even showing contempt for the public" (143). Quentin Tarantino famously weighed in at Cannes, saying that the director has "disappeared so far up his own ass that I have no desire to see another David Lynch movie" (Lynch and McKenna 310). There was a visceral reaction to *Fire Walk with Me*, sending Lynch the message, according to the director, that he had "killed *Twin Peaks* with this picture" (Rodley 189).

This phenomenon might be explained in part by the process by which adaptations can be perceived as "hideous progeny" (see Grossman, *Literature*). Viewers often turn away from adaptations in disgust because a changed source text disturbs viewers' stable sense of a story or text that has been internalized. The metaphor is drawn from Mary Shelley's description of her dream of Frankenstein's creature and the novel itself as "hideous progeny"; as anyone who has read the novel knows, however, the "monster" is more "human" than the creator. The significance of this for understanding adaptations and continuing stories is that they may have something more valuable and meaningful to say about their sources and contexts than viewers are initially ready to absorb. In this sense, television itself might be seen as monstrous in the way it has feverishly produced programming that creatively rewrites prior texts and genres (as in *The Bates Motel* [A&E, 2013–17], *Hannibal* [NBC, 2013–15], *Riverdale* [the CW, 2017-present], and *Penny Dreadful* [Showtime, 2014–16]), an idea that resonates with Sarah Cardwell's appreciation of TV as a "mongrel muse" (119). There is a way in which openness to new formulations of old stories challenges viewers to abandon control, perhaps analogously to the way both Cooper and the Log Lady associate death with "some fear in letting go." Requiring an openness on the part of viewers to appreciate major shifts in perspective on familiar and internalized stories and "home texts," *Fire Walk with Me* has been revalued in the years after its release, the *Village Voice* in 2013 calling it "David Lynch's masterpiece" (Marsh).

87

Despite the commercial motives for franchise storytelling, transmedia adaptations shift the agency of meaning from a single source (say, the 1990–91 television series *Twin Peaks*) to what emerges from a conversation among multiple paratexts, where the initial text recedes hierarchically in a new relay of textual relations. Watching *The Return*, for example, one wonders about Mr. C's insistence in Part 2 to Ray Monroe at the diner that he doesn't *need* anything: "Want, not need. I don't need anything, Ray. If there's one thing you should know about me, Ray, it's that I don't need anything. I want." Fueled by depraved appetite, or "want," the comment echoes *The Secret Diary*, in which Laura transcribes an exchange with BOB, who says, "I DON'T NEED ANYTHING [. . .] I WANT THINGS" (127).

As part of a continuing echoic dynamic, conversations among paratexts that build meaning are also constructed by viewers. It is, after all, not only the characters' "return" in the 2017 Showtime event but *ours* as well. Like the paratexts extending the world of *Twin Peaks*, our return to the show reshapes and recasts it with what is presumably a different affective bearing on the characters and stories, given our own and the performers' aging. Exceeding its fictionality, *The Return* keys actors' mortality and aging to our own, since it is the *real* bodies of performers previously playing familiar roles. Kyle MacLachlan, Sheryl Lee, Miguel Ferrer, Richard Beymer, Peggy Lipton, and others reappear twenty-five years after the original show to remind us that selves and texts are always moving in time. Perhaps this is why one of the most powerful scenes in *The Return* is Norma and Big Ed Hurley's final reunion in Part 15. Peggy Lipton recalls in *Room to Dream* that David Lynch stood on the side of the set "crying like a little baby" (Lynch and McKenna 481), as Otis Redding's song "I've Been Loving You Too Long" rang out. Aging Ed (with his usually bad "Hurley Luck" [Frost, *Final Dossier* 89, 90]) and stable, able, usually normal Norma resist the norm and strike a different path, claiming a happy ending. Conditioning us to rethink our ideas about fiction and realities that shift (and age) across time, *Twin Peaks* embodies an art that reminds us, as Mark Frost has said (in the voice of retiring journalist-editor Robert Jacoby in *The Final Dossier*), that "storytellers don't run out of stories; they just run out of time" (319).

Peggy Lipton as Norma Jennings, reuniting with Big Ed Hurley (Everett McGill) (*The Return*, Part 15).

The Return demonstrates the permeable contours of texts, since, as the 2017 "Twin Peaks" demonstrates, stories can never be fully told because elements refuse to be put to rest; they keep resurfacing in changed form, shifting like a cultural whack-a-mole. Even within the DVD and Blu-ray packaging of *Fire Walk with Me,* a kind of doubling of the film in its extras performs more "accretive extension" (Palmer 83) of the story. The discs include deleted and extended scenes and alternate takes from *Fire Walk with Me*, which Lynch edited in the order they might appear according to the film's narrative. Lynch thus provides an uncanny "twin film" in the home video extras, echoing the film and extending its textual borders.

This brief study of *Twin Peaks* has aimed to function similarly as paratextual prodding, giving us and hopefully our readers the opportunity to revisit, rethink, and reimagine a blended universe that continually reshapes our affective and critical responses to and interpretations of what we have watched. *Twin Peaks* compels its audiences to become part of a viewing experience nicely captured by Sarah Cardwell when she discusses the dynamism of "visual culture," which "implies something pervasive and encompassing—a context in which we live and participate rather than observe" (134). *Twin Peaks* is thoroughly committed to a world-building aesthetics that emphasizes the singularity of a fictional universe but also its openness to expansion and its belief in the values of blurred textual boundaries and fluid notions of identity. In active dialogue with its literary, filmic, and televisual continuations, "returns," and paratexts, *Twin Peaks* not only demonstrates the practice of remediation and transmedia storytelling but also contributes to advancing broad definitions of adaptation and its pleasures (like coffee and pie) and enduring significance in cultural production.

89

Episodes and Original Air Dates

Season 1 (ABC)

Pilot, "Northwest Passage" (April 8, 1990).
Written by Mark Frost and David Lynch. Directed by David Lynch.

Episode 1, "Traces to Nowhere" (April 12, 1990).
Written by Mark Frost and David Lynch. Directed by Duwayne
    Dunham.

Episode 2, "Zen, or the Skill to Catch a Killer" (April 19, 1990).
Written by Mark Frost and David Lynch. Directed by David Lynch.

Episode 3, "Rest in Pain" (April 26, 1990).
Written by Harley Peyton. Directed by Tina Rathborne.

Episode 4, "The One-Armed Man" (May 3, 1990).
Written by Robert Engels. Directed by Tim Hunter.

Episode 5, "Cooper's Dreams" (May 10, 1990).
Written by Mark Frost. Directed by Lesli Linka Glatter.

Episode 6, "Realization Time" (May 17, 1990).
Written by Harley Peyton. Directed by Caleb Deschanel.

Episode 7, "The Last Evening" (May 23, 1990).
Written and directed by Mark Frost.

Season 2 (ABC)

Episode 8, "May the Giant Be With You" (September 30, 1990).
Story by Mark Frost and David Lynch. Teleplay by Mark Frost. Directed
by David Lynch.

Episode 9, "Coma" (October 6, 1990).
Written by Harley Peyton. Directed by David Lynch.

Episode 10, "The Man Behind Glass" (October 13, 1990).
Written by Robert Engels. Directed by Lesli Linka Glatter.

Episode 11, "Laura's Secret Diary" (October 20, 1990).
Written by Jerry Stahl and Mark Frost and Harley Peyton and Robert
Engels. Directed by Tom Holland.

Episode 12, "The Orchid's Curse" (October 27, 1990).
Written by Barry Pullman. Directed by Graeme Clifford.

Episode 13, "Demons" (November 3, 1990).
Written by Harley Peyton and Robert Engels. Directed by Lesli Linka
Glatter.

Episode 14, "Lonely Souls" (November 10, 1990).
Written by Mark Frost. Directed by David Lynch.

Episode 15, "Drive with a Dead Girl" (November 17, 1990).
Written by Scott Frost. Directed by Caleb Deschanel.

Episode 16, "Arbitrary Law" (December 1, 1990).
Written by Mark Frost and Harley Peyton and Robert Engels. Directed by
Tim Hunter.

Episode 17, "Dispute between Brothers" (December 8, 1990).
Written by Tricia Brock. Directed by Tina Rathborne.

Episode 18, "Masked Ball" (December 15, 1990).
Written by Barry Pullman. Directed by Duwayne Dunham.

Episode 19, "The Black Widow" (January 12, 1991).
Written by Harley Peyton and Robert Engels. Directed by Caleb
Deschanel.

Episode 20, "Checkmate" (January 19, 1991).
Written by Harley Peyton. Directed by Todd Holland.

Episode 21, "Double Play" (February 2, 1991).
Written by Scott Frost. Directed by Uli Edel.

Episode 22, "Slaves and Masters" (February 9, 1991).
Written by Harley Peyton and Robert Engels. Directed by Diane Keaton.

Episode 23, "The Condemned Woman" (February 16, 1991).
Written by Tricia Brock. Directed by Lesli Linka Glatter.

Episode 24, "Wounds and Scars" (March 28, 1991).
Written by Barry Pullman. Directed by James Foley.

Episode 25, "On the Wings of Love" (April 4, 1991).
Written by Harley Peyton and Robert Engels. Directed by Duwayne Dunham.

Episode 26, "Variations on Relations" (April 11, 1991).
Written by Mark Frost and Harley Peyton. Directed by Jonathan Sanger.

Episode 27, "The Path to the Black Lodge" (April 18, 1991).
Written by Harley Peyton and Robert Engels. Directed by Stephen Gyllenhaal.

Episode 28, "Miss Twin Peaks" (June 10, 1991).
Written by Barry Pullman. Directed by Tim Hunter.

Episode 29, "Beyond Life and Death" (June 10, 1991).
Written by Mark Frost and Harley Peyton and Robert Engels. Directed by David Lynch.

The Return (Showtime, all cowritten by Mark Frost and David Lynch and directed by David Lynch)

Part 1, "My Log Has a Message For You" (May 21, 2017).

Part 2, "The Stars Turn and a Time Presents Itself" (May 21, 2017).

Part 3, "Call for Help" (May 28, 2017).

Part 4, ". . . Brings Back Some Memories" (May 28, 2017).

Part 5, "Case Files" (June 4, 2017).

Part 6, "Don't Die" (June 11, 2017).

Part 7, "There's a Body All Right" (June 18, 2017).

1 See Jowett for more on the roles of parody and homage in the afterlife of *Twin Peaks*.

2 The Salish Lodge and Spa in Snoqualmie doubled as the Great Northern Hotel, but the Great Northern's interiors were shot at the Kiana Lodge in Poulsbo. The exterior of the latter location served as the Martell home.

3 Packard, the maiden name of Laurie's character Catherine Martell, is also the surname of her character in *The Hustler*, Sarah Packard, as well as the boss of Lynch's father in Boise, Idaho, when he worked for the US Department of Agriculture (Lynch and McKenna 23).

4 For a comprehensive mapping of the intertextual references in the series, see Halskov 146–51. According to his interview with Caleb Deschanel, director of Episodes 6, 15, and 19, Frost was conscious of film and television citations in the larger story and discussed them with Deschanel, but Lynch was tight-lipped about the intertextuality.

5 For further investigations of this phenomenon, see: Hayes and Boulègue; Halskov; Hills; Jenkins; and R. Williams. See also Smith, Goddard, and Fairclough for a special issue of the journal *Series* dedicated to the fan cultures of *Twin Peaks*.

6 See Lim for a critical biography of Lynch, and Todd for a study of his reputation. Both writers address the relationship between his status as an auteur and his public image.

7 See Ayers for more on melodrama and the "sincere emotional engagement" (95) of *Twin Peaks*. For more on the series as a soap opera, see Halskov and Linda Ruth Williams.

8 See Naremore, *More than Night,* for more on noir as a "mediascape" rather than as a category of films alone.

9 See also Reeves et al. for a discussion of *Twin Peaks* in the context of postmodernism and television.

10 For an excellent discussion of race, place, and nation, which indirectly touches on the western location, see Guan.

11 Tim Hunter, a self-identified "film buff," has acknowledged the influence of film noir and the Technicolor melodramas of Sirk and Vincente Minnelli on the episodes he directed (Episodes 4, 16, and 28). See Halskov 148–49.

12 Fenn went on to play Elizabeth Taylor in the made-for-television film *Liz: The Elizabeth Taylor Story* (NBC, 1995), and Tamblyn reprised his character for three episodes of *General Hospital* in 2000.

13 For an in-depth analysis of Angelo Badalamenti's score, see Norelli.

14 The real house is located in Everett, Washington, and the real owner (as of 2014) plays Alice Tremond in Part 18 (Ivie). Lynch used this same house for *Twin Peaks: Fire Walk with Me* and the pilot. A different house located in Monroe, Washington, was used for exterior shots in the first two seasons.

15 See Scheibel for a similar argument about Lynch's *Mulholland Drive*.

16 See Martin for a larger discussion of Lynch's use of architecture and design in *Twin Peaks*.

17 See Thain for a reading of the "dance moves" in *Twin Peaks*.

18 See Hallam, *Twin Peaks*, for more on this idea.

19 Thomas Leitch wonders, indeed, if "all adaptations are performances" ("Adaptation and Intertextuality" 99), and, in an intriguing related discussion, Kyle Meikle demonstrates how adaptations provide a "unique series of interactivities," including between "old materials and new, old media and new" (555).

WORKS CITED

Abbott, Stacey. "'Doing Weird Things for the Sake of Being Weird': Directing *Twin Peaks*." Weinstock and Spooner, pp. 175–91.

Advertisement for *Twin Peaks*. *New York Times*, 8 Apr. 1990, p. H30.

Ang, Ien. *Watching* Dallas*: Soap Opera and the Melodramatic Imagination*. Translated by Della Couling, Routledge, 1989.

Ansen, David. "The Kid from Mars." *Newsweek*, 9 Apr. 1990, pp. 66–71.

Ayers, Sheli. "*Twin Peaks*, Weak Language and the Resurrection of Affect." Sheen and Davison, pp. 93–106.

Barney, Richard, editor. *David Lynch: Interviews*. University of Mississippi Press, 2009,

Bolter, Jay David, and Richard Grusin. *Remediation: Understanding New Media*. MIT Press, 1999.

Bordwell, David. "The Art Cinema as a Mode of Film Practice." *Film Criticism*, vol. 4, no. 1, 1979, pp. 56–64.

Breskin, David. "The *Rolling Stone* Interview with David Lynch." *Rolling Stone*, 6 Sep. 1990, pp. 58–63, 98–100.

Bushman, David, and Mark Givens. "The Real Mystery of *Twin Peaks*: Who Killed Hazel Drew?" *Washington Post*, 14 May 2017, p. E1.

Canby, Vincent. "One Long Last Gasp for Laura Palmer." *New York Times*, 29 Aug. 1992, p. 11.

Cardwell, Sarah. "A *Dickensian* Feast: Visual Culture and Television Aesthetics." Grossman and Palmer, pp. 119–37.

Carlson, Timothy. "Welcome to the Weird, New World of *Twin Peaks*." *TV Guide*, 7 Apr. 1990, pp. 20–23.

Carroll, Michael. "Agent Cooper's Errand in the Wilderness: *Twin Peaks* and American Mythology." *Literature/Film Quarterly*, vol. 21, no. 4, 1993, pp. 287–95.

Carter, Bill. "*Twin Peaks* May Provide a Ratings Edge for ABC." *New York Times*, 16 Apr. 1990, p. D8.

Chion, Michel. *David Lynch*. Translated by Robert Julian, BFI, 1995.

Ciment, Michel, and Hubert Niogret. "Interview with David Lynch." Barney, pp. 106–24.

Collins, Jim. "Television and Postmodernism." *Channels of Discourse, Reassembled: Television and Contemporary Criticism*. 2nd ed., edited by Robert C. Allen, University of North Carolina Press, pp. 327–53.

Corliss, Richard. "Czar of Bizarre." *Time*, 1 Oct. 1990, pp. 84–89.

Dyer, Richard. *Stars*. 2nd ed., BFI, 1998.

Elm, Joanna. "Whodunit?: Four Top Authors Solve the *Twin Peaks* Mystery." *TV Guide*, 8 Sep. 1990, pp. 2–4, 6.

Evans, Peter William. "*Double Indemnity* (or Bringing Up Baby)." *The Book of Film Noir*, edited by Ian Cameron, Continuum, 1993, pp. 165–73.

Frost, Mark. *The Secret History of Twin Peaks*. Flatiron Books, 2016.

———. *Twin Peaks: The Final Dossier*. Flatiron Books, 2017.

Frost, Mark, David Lynch, and Richard Saul Wurman. *Welcome to Twin Peaks: Access Guide to the Town*. Access Press, 1991.

Frost, Scott. *The Autobiography of F.B.I. Special Agent Dale Cooper: My Life, My Tapes*. Penguin, 1991.

George, Diana Hume. "Lynching Women: A Feminist Reading of *Twin Peaks*." Lavery, 109–19.

Gerard, Jeremy. "A 'Soap Noir' Inspires a Cult and Questions." *New York Times*, 26 Apr. 1990, p. C22.

Grant, Barry Keith. *Film Genre: From Iconography to Ideology*. Wallflower, 2007.

Grossman, Julie. *Literature, Film, and Their Hideous Progeny: Adaptation and ElasTEXTity*. Palgrave, 2015.

———. *Rethinking the Femme Fatale in Film Noir: Ready for Her Closeup*. 2009. Palgrave, 2012.

Grossman, Julie, and R. Barton Palmer, editors. *Adaptation in Visual Culture: Images, Texts, and Their Multiple Worlds*. Palgrave, 2017.

Guan, Frank. "What Does David Lynch Have to Say About Race?" *Vulture*, 12 Sep. 2017, http://www.vulture.com/2017/09/david-lynch-racial-politics.html. Accessed 29 Aug. 2019.

Hallam, Lindsay. "May the Giant Be with You: *Twin Peaks* Season Two, Episode One and the Television Auteur." *Senses of Cinema*, no. 79, 2016, http://sensesofcinema.com/2016/twin-peaks/lynch-televison-auteur/. Accessed 7 Jul. 2018.

————. *Twin Peaks: Fire Walk with Me*. Auteur Publishing, 2018.

Halskov, Andreas. *TV Peaks and Modern Television Drama*. University of Southern Denmark Press, 2015.

Hayes, Marisa C., and Franck Boulègue. *Fan Phenomena: Twin Peaks*. Intellect, 2013.

Hills, Matt. "'I'll See You Again in 25 Years': Paratextually Re-commodifying and Revisiting Anniversary *Twin Peaks*." Weinstock and Spooner, pp. 193–209.

Hoberman, J., and Jonathan Rosenbaum. *Midnight Movies*. 1983. Da Capo P, 1991.

Hughes, David. *The Complete Lynch*. Virgin, 2001.

Hutcheon, Linda. *A Theory of Adaptation*. Routledge, 2006.

Hutcheon, Linda, and Gary R. Bortolotti. "On the Origin of Adaptations: Rethinking Fidelity Discourse and 'Success'—Biologically." *New Literary History*, vol. 38, no. 3, 2007, pp. 443–58.

Ivie, Devon. "How the Laura Palmer House's Actual Owner Ended Up in Twin Peaks: The Return's Final Scene." *Vulture*, 19 Sep. 2017, http://www.vulture.com/2017/09/twin-peaks-laura-palmer-house-real-homeowner-mary-reber.html. Accessed 29 Aug. 2018.

Jenkins, Henry. "'Do You Enjoy Making the Rest of Us Feel Stupid?': alt.tv.twinpeaks, the Trickster Author, and Viewer Mastery." Lavery, pp. 51–69.

Jensen, Jeff. "Peaks 'n' Freaks." *Entertainment Weekly*, 31 Mar. 2017, pp. 20–27, 29.

Jerome, Jim. "The Triumph of Twin Peaks." *Entertainment Weekly*, 6 Apr. 1990, pp. 34–38, 40, 42.

Jowett, Lorna. "Nightmare in Red?: *Twin Peaks* Parody, Homage, Intertextuality, and Mashup." Weinstock and Spooner, pp. 211–27.

Jowett, Lorna, and Stacey Abbott. *TV Horror: Investigating the Dark Side of the Small Screen*. I.B. Tauris, 2013.

Kalinak, Kathryn. "'Disturbing the Guests with This Racket': Music and *Twin Peaks*." Lavery, pp. 82–92.

Kapsis, Robert. *Hitchcock: The Making of a Reputation*. University of Chicago Press, 1992.

Lacey, Stephen. "Just Plain Odd: Some Thoughts on Performance Styles in *Twin Peaks*." *Cinema Journal*, vol. 55, no. 3, Spring 2016, pp. 126–31.

Lafky, Sue. "Gender, Power, and Culture in the Televisual World of *Twin Peaks*: A Feminist Critique." *Journal of Film and Video*, vol. 51, no. 3/4, pp. 5–19.

Lavery, David, editor. *Full of Secrets: Critical Approaches to* Twin Peaks. Wayne State University Press, 1995.

Lavery, David. "Introduction: The Semiotics of Cobbler: *Twin Peaks*' Interpretive Community." Lavery, pp. 1–21.

Leerhsen, Charles, with Lynda Wright. "Psychic Moms and Cherry Pie." *Newsweek*, 7 May 1990, pp. 58–59.

Leitch, Thomas. "Adaptation and Intertextuality, or, What isn't an Adaptation, and What Does it Matter?" *A Companion to Literature, Film, and Adaptation*, edited by Deborah Cartmell, Blackwell, 2012, pp. 87–104.

———. "Mind the Gaps." Grossman and Palmer, 53–72.

———. *The Oxford Handbook of Adaptation Studies*. Edited by Thomas Leitch, Oxford University Press, 2017.

———. "To Adapt or To Adapt To: Consequences of Approaching Film Adaptation Intransitively." *Studia Filmoznawcze*, 30, 2009, pp. 91–103.

Leonard, John. "The Quirky Allure of *Twin Peaks*." *New York*, 7 May 1990, pp. 32–39.

Lim, Dennis. *David Lynch: The Man From Another Place*. Houghton Mifflin Harcourt, 2015.

Lucas, Tim. "One Chance Out Between Two Worlds: Notes on *Twin Peaks—Fire Walk with Me*." *Video Watchdog*, no. 16, 1993, pp. 28–47.

Lynch, David, and Kristine McKenna. *Room to Dream*. Random House, 2018.

Lynch, Jennifer. *The Secret Diary of Laura Palmer*. New York: Pocket Books, 1990.

MacCannell, Dean. "Marilyn Monroe Was Not a Man." *Diacritics*, vol. 17, no. 2, 1987, pp. 114–27.

Marcus, Greil. *The Shape of Things to Come: Prophecy and the American Voice*. Farrar, Strauss and Giroux, 2006.

"Mark Frost Interview With *Wrapped in Plastic*." *Twin Peaks: The Entire Mystery*. Paramount and CBS Blu-ray, 2014.

Marsh, Calum. "*Twin Peaks: Fire Walk with Me* Is David Lynch's Masterpiece." *Village Voice*, 17 May 2013, https://www.villagevoice.com/2013/05/17/twin-peaks-fire-walk-with-me-is-david-lynchs-masterpiece/. Accessed 30 Aug. 2018.

Martin, Richard. *The Architecture of David Lynch*. Bloomsbury, 2014.

McGowan, Todd. *The Impossible David Lynch*. Columbia University Press, 2007.

Meikle, Kyle. "Adaptation and Interactivity." Leitch, *Oxford Handbook*, pp. 542–56.

Mittell, Jason. "Narrative Complexity in Contemporary American Television." *The Velvet Light Trap*, no. 58, 2006, pp. 29–40.

Mulvey, Laura. "Visual Pleasure and Narrative Cinema." *Screen*, vol. 16, no. 3, 1975, pp. 6–18.

Murray, S. "*Twin Peaks: Fire Walk with Me*: The Press Conference at Cannes 1992." Barney, pp. 134–44.

Naremore, James. *Acting in the Cinema*. University of California Press, 1988.

———. *More than Night: Film Noir in Its Contexts*. 2nd ed., University of California Press, 2008.

Neale, Steve. "Melodrama and Tears." *Screen*, vol. 27, no. 6, 1986, pp. 6–22.

Nieland, Justus. *David Lynch*. University of Illinois Press, 2013.

Nochimson, Martha. "Desire Under the Douglas Firs: Entering the Body of Reality in *Twin Peaks*." Lavery, pp. 144–59.

Norelli, Clare Nina. *Soundtrack From Twin Peaks*. Bloomsbury, 2017.

Ochoa, Laurie. "Coffee Shops Jump the *Twin Peaks* Bandwagon." *Houston Chronicle*, 17 Oct. 1990, p. 9.

O'Falt, Chris. "*Twin Peaks*: Mark Frost Takes Us Inside the Four-Year Process of Writing a 500-Page Script Over Skype with David Lynch." *IndieWire*, 14 June 2018, https://www.indiewire.com/2018/06/twin-peaks-the-return-mark-frost-david-lynch-writing-collaboration-1201975099/. Accessed 29 Aug. 2018.

Palmer, R. Barton. "Continuation, Adaptation Studies, and the Never-Finished Text." Grossman and Palmer, pp. 73–100.

Pond, Steve. "Naked Lynch." *Rolling Stone*, 22 Mar. 1990, pp. 51–54, 120.

Pollack, Andrew. "*Twin Peaks* Mania Peaks in Japan." *New York Times*, 2 Aug. 1992, p. 18.

"Postcards from the Cast." *Twin Peaks: The Entire Mystery*. Paramount and CBS Blu-ray, 2014.

Ramsay, Christine. "*Twin Peaks*: Mountains or Molehills?" *CineAction!*, no. 24/25, 1991, pp. 50–59.

Reeves, Jimmie L., et al. "Postmodernism and Television: Speaking of *Twin Peaks*." Lavery, pp. 173–95.

Richardson, John. "*Laura* and *Twin Peaks*: Postmodern Parody and the Musical Reconstruction of the Absent Femme Fatale." Sheen and Davison, pp. 77–92.

Rodley, Chris. *Lynch on Lynch*. 1997. Farrar, Strauss and Giroux, 2005.

Ryan, Marie-Laure. "Transmedia Storytelling as Narrative Practice." Leitch, *Oxford Handbook*, pp. 527–41.

Ryan, Maureen. "Peak Performance." *Variety*, vol. 336, no. 1, 9 May 2017, pp. 40–47.

Scheibel, Will. "A Fallen Star Over *Mulholland Drive*: Representation of the Actress." *Film Criticism*, vol. 42, no. 1, 2018, http://dx.doi.org/10.3998/fc.13761232.0042.107.

Schrader, Paul. "Notes on Film Noir." *Film Noir Reader*, edited by Alain Silver and James Ursini, Limelight Editions, 1996, pp. 53–63.

"Secrets From Another Place: Creating *Twin Peaks*." *Twin Peaks: The Entire Mystery*. Paramount and CBS Blu-ray, 2014.

Self, Robert T. "Resisting Reality: Acting by Design in Robert Altman's *Nashville*." *More Than a Method: Trends and Traditions in Contemporary Film Performance*, edited by Cynthia Baron, Diane Carson, and Frank P. Tomasulo, Wayne State University Press, 2004, pp. 126–50.

Shales, Tom. "The Moody Man of *Twin Peaks*." *Washington Post*, 6 Apr. 1990, pp. C1, C8.

Sheen, Erica, and Annette Davison, editors. *The Cinema of David Lynch: American Dreams, Nightmare Visions*. Wallflower, 2004.

Smith, Anthony N., Michael Goddard, and Kirsty Fairclough, editors. *Series: International Journal of TV Serial Narratives*, vol. 11, no. 2, 2016.

Smith, Michael Glover. "Director David Lynch on Meditation, Creativity, and Twin Peaks." *Time Out*, 20 Sep. 2016, https://www.timeout.com/usa/blog/director-david-lynch-on-meditation-creativity-and-twin-peaks-092016. Accessed 14 Jul. 2018.

Sobchack, Vivian. "Lounge Time: Postwar Crisis and the Chronotope of Film Noir." *Refiguring American Film Genres: Theory and History*, edited by Nick Browne, University of California Press, 1998, pp. 129–70.

Sobran, Joseph. "Weird American." *National Review*, 1 Oct. 1990, pp. 38–40.

Taubin, Amy. "Cheers It Ain't." *Village Voice*, 10 Apr. 1990, pp. 32–36.

Telotte, J. P. "'Complementary Verses': The Science Fiction of *Twin Peaks*." Weinstock and Spooner, pp. 161–74.

Thain, Alanna. "One Way Out Between Two Worlds: The Dance Moves of Twin Peaks." *Senses of Cinema*, no. 79, 2016, http://sensesofcinema.com/2016/twin-peaks/dance-in-twin-peaks/. Accessed 26 Jul. 2018.

Thompson, Kristin. *Storytelling in Film and Television*. Harvard University Press, 2003.

Thompson, Robert J. *Television's Second Golden Age: From* Hill Street Blues *to* ER. Syracuse University Press, 1996.

Tobias, Scott, et al. "20 TV Shows Most Influenced by *Twin Peaks*." *Rolling Stone*, 16 May 2017, https://www.rollingstone.com/tv/tv-lists/

20-tv-shows-most-influenced-by-twin-peaks-126797/bates-motel -114269/. Accessed 1 Sep. 2018.

Todd, Antony. *Authorship and the Films of David Lynch: Aesthetic Reception in Contemporary Hollywood*. I. B. Tauris, 2012.

Tucker, Ken. "*Twin Peaks*." *Entertainment Weekly*, 6 Apr. 1990, pp. 6–8, 11.

Tusher, Will. "Kurosawa to Join Other Winners at Asian/Pacific Jimmie Awards." *Variety*, 28 Jan. 1991, p. 18.

Verevis, Constantine. "The Cinematic Return." *Film Criticism*, vol. 40, no.1, 2016, https://quod.lib.umich.edu/f/fc/13761232.0040.134/-cinematic -return?rgn=main;view=fulltext;q1=Verevis.

Wallace, David Foster. "David Lynch Keeps His Head." *A Supposedly Fun Thing I'll Never Do Again: Essays and Arguments*, Little, Brown and Company, 1997, pp. 146–212.

Weinstein, Steve. "Is Television Ready for David Lynch?" *Los Angeles Times*, 18 Feb. 1990, pp. N8, 92.

Weinstock, Andrew, and Catherine Spooner, editors. *Return to* Twin Peaks: *New Approaches to Materiality, Theory, and Genre on Television*. Palgrave, 2016.

White, Mimi. "Television Genres: Intertextuality." *Journal of Film and Video*, vol. 37, no. 3, 1985, pp. 41–47.

Williams, Linda. "Film Bodies: Gender, Genre, and Excess." *Film Quarterly*, vol. 44, no. 4, 1991, pp. 2–13.

Williams, Linda Ruth. "*Twin Peaks*: David Lynch and the Serial-Thriller Soap." *The Contemporary Television Series*, edited by Michael Hammond and Lucy Mazdon, Edinburgh University Press, 2005, pp. 37–56.

Williams, Rebecca. "Ontological Security, Authorship, and Resurrection: Exploring *Twin Peaks*' Social Media Afterlife." *Cinema Journal*, vol. 55, no. 3, 2016, pp. 143–47.

Woodward, Richard M. "A Dark Lens on America." *New York Times Magazine*, 14 Jan. 1990, pp. 19–21, 30, 42–43, 52.

———. "When *Blue Velvet* Meets *Hill Street Blues*." *New York Times*, 8 Apr. 1990, p. 31.

Zehme, Bill. "Babes in the Woods: Sharing Pie and Secrets with the Mystery Girls of *Twin Peaks*." *Rolling Stone*, 4 Oct. 1990, pp. 68–72, 170.

Zoglin, Richard. "Like Nothing on Earth." *Time*, 9 Apr. 1990, pp. 96–97.

———. "A Sleeper with a Dream." *Time*, 21 May 1990, pp. 86–87.

ABOUT THE AUTHORS

JULIE GROSSMAN is professor of English and communication and film studies at Le Moyne College in Syracuse, New York. Her books include *Rethinking the Femme Fatale in Film Noir: Ready for Her Close-Up*; *Literature, Film, and Their Hideous Progeny: Adaptation and ElasTEXTity*; and *Ida Lupino, Director: Her Art and Resilience in Times of Transition* (with Therese Grisham). She is co-editor with R. Barton Palmer of the book series *Adaptation and Visual Culture* and the collection *Adaptation in Visual Culture: Images, Texts, and Their Multiple Worlds*.

WILL SCHEIBEL is associate professor in the Department of English at Syracuse University, where he teaches film and screen studies, and is affiliated with the Goldring Arts Journalism Program. He is the author of *American Stranger: Modernisms, Hollywood, and the Cinema of Nicholas Ray* and, with Steven Rybin, co-editor of *Lonely Places, Dangerous Ground: Nicholas Ray in American Cinema*.